Dedication

To
Joan Holmes
The Executive Director of The Hunger Project
For her fierce, unyielding intention that hunger shall end
by 1997.

to
Werner Erhard
For his unceasing work to make transformation real.

to
Richard M. De Vos and Jay Van Andel
For lighting the way of transformation in business.

to
My son Houston
whose entire future lies in front of him
and my wife Jean
who gave him life.

This volume is to be read after
Winning Through Enlightenment.

TRANSFORMING #1

Ron Smothermon, M.D.

Context Publications

San Francisco

ISBN 0-932654-04-5
Library of Congress catalog card number 81-14356

Acknowledgements

This book is, as was *Winning Through Enlightenment*, a synthesis from many sources and is not intended to accurately represent any source or any point of view other than my own. Nevertheless, some individuals have contributed so much to my life and to my ability to think creatively, that not to mention them would simply be inappropriate. In my experience, Werner Erhard has stated the principles of transformation so clearly that anyone who is awake can, as Werner likes to say, "get it." Vern Black has done seminal work with the states of integrity and his friendship has lent reality to the ideas he has created. Vic Baronco and Justin Sterling are two magnificent individuals who are working independent of each other, yet reaching many of the same conclusions about the mysteries of man/woman relationships. Francis Moore Lappé and Joseph Collins have done remarkable research into the conditions holding world hunger in place and while we differ in some very important ways, the quality of their work is an inspiration to me. Rich De Vos and Jay Van Andel created transformation in business through founding a transformed corporation long before the word "transformation" became popular. And finally the fiery intention of Joan Holmes, the Executive Director of The Hunger Project, is a flame in my heart in which I bask on a daily basis.

Ron Smothermon, M.D.
San Francisco

Preface

Over three years have passed since I began writing *Winning Through Enlightenment*. In that time most of my energy has gone toward publishing that book and seeing it into the market place. It has been an interesting and educational process for me to publish *WTE*, fully as big a job as writing it in the first place.

Almost from the beginning, those around me have urged, even insisted, that I write again. I have resisted that temptation until it became clear to me that *Winning Through Enlightenment* would reach the readers who might be interested in it, and that it would realize its intended results, namely the experience of Empowered Self. For me, that book is complete, even as it begins to arrive on the market place and its whole, entire future lies ahead of it. This frees me to write to you again. The miracles which have occurred in the lives of people who have read *WTE* have liberated me and empowered me as a writer and as a human being. It is now absolutely the truth for me that life is a place where miracles happen and that we only need to be alive to discover that.

I want to share with you the joy I have in writing this book to you and I want you to know that I have a direct experience of writing this to *you*, and that this experience of you and me is an experience of relationship which endures through all time, transcending events, memory, forgetfulness, and even time itself. When I write to you, your divinity becomes real for me.

Table of Contents

BOOK I
TRANSFORMATION OF
SELF

This book is about transforming yourself, not about changing yourself. The nature of transformation is that it is always complete, so there is nothing for you to do. You can only transform that which is already transformed. Self is, and always was, transformed. Therefore, transforming your Self is complete, and a certain characteristic of your transformation is that you carry it into the world.

Chapter One:
Transformation

Your transformation is at hand.

"Transformation" is the word I use to describe what this book is about. Technically, the word itself is incorrect since it refers to a change in form and this book is not about a change in form, but rather a change in value. "Transvaluation" is a better word and it is not accepted in our language. Transformation is not about making life "better," but rather it is about creating value in life *as it is*, which includes the fact that life is changing.

Everyone I know is committed to her own transformation, without exception. That is to say, everyone is committed to having the experience of expanded value in his life. Some realize that what that means is transformation of the quality of all lives and others think they can transform the quality of one life and not all others. Nevertheless, everyone I have known has been committed to her own transformation. Some think that increased quality means increased quantity and others realize that quality and quantity exist in separate realms. Nevertheless, all are committed to transformation. And some think transformation can be legislated or forced upon others while a few know that it is a function of creation, not force or legislation. Nevertheless, everyone I know is totally committed to his own transformation. In short, the search for transformation is a universal human attribute, even though in the usual course of events the direction of the search turns out to be a joke for most of humanity.

When you bring up the word "love" with people you will find

5

that everyone is searching for a definition. Someone told me recently that love is honesty, another said love is support and the willingness to be supported, another said love is the willingness to
allow others to be the way they are and the way they are not (that
is, if they change it is OK). I must admit that the definitions are
creative and useful at times, although very misleading. Misleading
because no definition holds. Love can exist in the absence of honesty, support, and willingness, and anything else you can name. This
is because love is not a "thing" and definitions hold only for things.
A non-thing cannot be defined in words, since words can apply only to things. Transformation fits into this category: it is a non-thing.
You cannot transform a thing and no thing can transform you.
Also, transformation does not exist in time like "things." Nor is it
found in a particular place as are all things. When you picked up
this book you probably thought of transformation as happiness or
joy or a "peak experience." Happiness, joy, and peak experiences
do occur and they are great, and they are not transformation, for
they are events and occur in time. Transformation is not an event
and it occurs out of time.

When you realize that love *is*, not is a particular thing, but
simply *is*, then you can have love and you realize that you have
always had love, blocking the experience merely by searching for
"it" as if it were an "it," a thing (a feeling). So what you can say
about love is "Love is" and that is all you can say without lying.
Just as obviously, transformation *is* and that is all you can say
about it without lying.

So if transformation is, then what is transformed? Obviously
things are not transformed by a non-thing. Only another non-thing
could be transformed by a non-thing. I term this non-thing Self, or
Empowered Self, "Self" for short. Self *is* transformation and it
could be said that actually Self has always been transformed, that
you can only transform that which is transformed.

The word "Self" is quite useful since it puts you in touch with
your true nature, Who You Are, and this is not accomplished by
any of the terms which refer to things such as "body," "mind,"
"personality," "ego," and so forth. Obviously I am not my personality any more than I am my left foot. I could do without either,
that is easy to see. It is not so obvious that I can do without my
body. We are so identified with our bodies that it is impossible to

fully know that we survive without our bodies. Some of us are so identified with our car, or our house, or our spouse, or our jewels that we find it practically impossible to know that we survive without those things. If I beat up your new car, you would think you just died and after that you would do something to me to make me think that I had just died. We are attached to "things" and amongst things is the Mind. It is this attachment to Mind as Self which keeps one stuck chasing happiness rather than having it. Transformation fundamentally alters that. Remember that transformation is, however that does not mean you are in touch with transformation. The purpose of this book is for you to put yourself in touch with your transformation.

I love the use of a flash of lightning to represent transformation. As lightning is frozen in time by the photographer and the camera, so is transformation frozen out of time, for all time, by Self. As lightning is illuminating, so is transformation. If you have eyes, look. If you have ears, listen, for your transformation is at hand.

Chapter Two:
A Mythology Of Beginnings

"I'll send them one crummy example of what a human being could be."

This is a story about you before you were born, before you were conceived, before your mother and father thought about you or knew each other. It is also a story about you after your body has given up the struggle to live, after the particles of your physicality have become one with the universe again. It is a story about you right now, in this instant, and it is a story about your past and your future. It is a story about the time in your life and about transcending time with its linear sequence of events.

To begin, let me tell you a story, a metaphor, a myth. In the beginning was Self, and Self was one with the universe, and Self *was* the universe, being everything simultaneously. Self became interested and enthusiastic about making up some trouble and at that moment the first living molecule came into being. Self then occupied time by rearranging molecules and this amused Self for millions and millions of years. And then Self became interested and enthusiastic about making up more trouble and evolution began. Much to Self's surprise evolution produced interested and enthusiastic creatures whose interest and enthusiasm were focused on making up trouble. And these creatures eventually began to communicate freely with each other and Self watched with great interest and enthusiasm.

And, as Self watched, she had a sudden realization of seeing herself in each creature and said, "I will make a creature truly capable of interest, enthusiasm and trouble-making." And evolution accelerated. Out of nothing came man and woman. Self looked at her many complete representations and realized the potential for trouble. "I have made a terrible mistake," she thought and she tried to communicate with her individual carbon-based units to correct the mistake. But they repeatedly misunderstood her statements and eventually she gave up and in her wisdom buried her mistake *by becoming the mistake and living within each individual*. And civilization advanced rapidly.

The game of Self then became to discover herself and experience herself as she had before time and all this trouble began. To make the game interesting, she told no one. "Let them guess," she thought as she became more firmly grounded in each individual and her thoughts blended with the thoughts of her creatures. "Let life be a game wherein the rules state that it is not a game," she said. And it was so. "Let some be persecutors and others be persecuted," she thought, and it came to pass. "Some will be helpers in all this mess and others will be helped," and it was so. "Let there be war, starvation, killing, loving, hating, and great diseases to overcome," and it was so. "Let the object of the game be to get out of this mess and I'll send them one crummy example of what a human being could be to tantalize them. Let the game begin." And the game began in a giant orchestration. This is your story. You are that one crummy example of what a human being could be. Self created Self.

Chapter Three:
Go Forth Into The World

Self set you forth in a world seemingly bound in the confines of time. She became you and you were perfect.

When Empowered Self said, "I'll send them one crummy example of what a human being could be to tantalize them," you had your beginnings. This was your pre-biological beginning, when you were a thought without a form. Self then sent you into the world to represent Her; a formless thought became form, a body and a mind. To bring this into being Self selected two human beings by having them select each other and by blessing them with bodies capable of reproduction. The cells were mixed and your body is the result, a carbon-based unit unlike any other. In the early months Self supplied you with an environment which closely approximated the comfort experienced by Empowered Self, but then you were expelled from the womb in the most traumatic event of your life. Thus were you initiated into your opportunity to be that one crummy example of what a human being could be. And your first barrier (without which there would be no game) was the physical discomfort of being physical, and of being born.

But the pain was not bad in those early years, for you only had to consume adequate food to remain fairly comfortable. Not only that, you had special adults around you who took it as their job in life to see that you were comfortable and, in those days, you knew your own magnificence. You were naturally enthusiastic and interested in life. You were capable of creating any thought and of wondering any wonder, and you did both constantly. You caused your daily life to happen by magic. By magic you were fed, by magic you could see and hear, by magic you slept, by magic you awoke, by magic you were loved and by magic you loved others. Nothing was unnatural in those times: there was no pretense, there was no hating, there was no depression. Life was a dream wherein you were the dreamer. And She was pleased, for Empowered Self recognized in you that one crummy example of what a human being could be.

This game was set forth in time, that is existing with a beginning, a middle, and an end in relationship to other beginnings, middles, and ends. So Empowered Self, who exists independent of the illusion of time, set you forth as an example in a world bound in the confines of time. She became you and you were perfect.

Chapter Four:
In the Middle Of It All

*You believed, and in believing you fell from
your natural grace.*

Before you arrived in the world as an individual, you had
already arrived in the world as millions of individuals. You had
created a world to receive you, wherein you could play out your
game in life under difficult rules and circumstances. You prepared
for yourself, over the millenia, a world in which, not only is there
war and murder, but a world in which the supposed cure for war
and murder is more war and murder. You founded a world complete with an abundance of food wherein people starve to death at a
phenomenal rate. For yourself you prepared a place in which your
gain could only come at the expense of someone else's loss. And, to
make the game ultimately difficult for yourself, you have denied
your responsibility in having created it all the way it is. You have
placed yourself at the bottom of the ladder—you found the world
this way and are victimized by it.

So, the challenge was complete and you passed from the beginning to the middle in life. The transition occurred when you left
behind the experience of a magical life and listened to someone's explanation of it, which you believed, and in believing you fell from
your natural grace. Self continued to see in you that one crummy
example for the world, even as you let go of Who You Are and
began to believe your beliefs. You sold out.

You believed..."Suffering is inevitable"...you believed..."I
must love my parents"...you believed..."It is wrong to think the

thoughts I think"...you believed..."There is a set of rules around here, if I could just find them everything would be OK"...you believed..."They have been around here longer than I have, they must know what the rules are"...you believed..."Everything must have a rational explanation"...you believed..."I am right about everything"...you believed..."I have to pretend in order to get through this world." And on. The point is that you gave up your magical experience of life and believed. Now you believe in place of being.

The game then became to see if you could make it through life and find some sense of satisfaction after having given up your ability to make it effortlessly and having given up your natural sense of satisfaction. This then, is the middle of the game. Welcome to the middle. Welcome to the challenge you have created through your world and through your adaptation to your world.

Chapter Five:
The Resistance Game

What we call "life" is a game of wishing what is and is not to exchange places.

Having spoken of the beginning and the middle, it is only completion to speak of the end of the game. Death, or the end of the game, has preoccupied people forever. Recent books forward the idea that at the moment of death the spirit leaves the body and begins a process of discovery leading ultimately to heaven, hell, or rebirth, depending on whose writing you read. Obviously, none of the writers have actually died and come back to tell of their experience, or if they have they cannot prove it. Those who presumably died cannot be known to have had all of their brain cells extinguished and as far as I am concerned, from a scientific standpoint, we are as far away from having hard evidence about what experience one has, if any, after all brain cells are extinguished as we ever were. It is important to understand that intracellular chemical processes proceed after no external cell life can be observed.

So I want to speak to you of death in a responsible way and not assume that something is true for which I have no evidence, scientific or experiential. Rather, I want to see if we have any way of looking at the end of the game which is both true and supports the game in present time.

There are two ways of looking at matter. One is that there is a division between living and non-living matter. This presumes that some matter, such as your body, has a quality which other matter, such as a rock, does not have. Matter could be said to be defined by the quality of being physical, in fact your body and a rock share this quality. Presumably your body differs from a rock by having the ability to act. However, as we have probed into the nature of atomic structure we have discovered that matter both thinks and acts and, at the level of the atom, all matter is living. There is no such thing as non-living matter! Only the form of the expression in thinking and acting distinguishes your body from a rock. So matter itself is alive, and this is the second way of looking at matter.

Given the above, what distinguishes the "life" of our Mind/body from the "life" of a rock? The only substantial difference, as I see it, is that Mind (includes body) "hopes" that the physical arrangement of atoms within it will not change and a rock does not so hope. A rock accepts the inevitability of change and Mind does not, and that is the only difference. Otherwise there is no fundamental difference. You might say then that a mind is a resistance machine whose job it is to resist the inevitability of change.

Now, most of what we would like to preserve, that is, what we call "consciousness" is, in fact, nothing but resistance to the laws of nature. A rock does not worry about dying. Human beings do. Human beings then, are physical things which have devised a resistance game to play, one rule of said game being not to call it a game and another rule is to "hope" that the inevitable change of form is not inevitable, that is to wish what is to be what is not. And this is the grist of "life" as we define it.

So, what happens with "death?" What happens is that the game ends. That is it and that is all there is, as far as we know. All the rest is speculation.

So what about Empowered Self? Perhaps you thought She was a human being. Most people seem to think that. However that thought is simply part of the resistance game we call "life." Empowered Self *is* Life in the broadest sense of the word, not the narrow sense you have for it. Self is just as pleased to empower a rock as she is to empower your resistance survival game. Only from your wishful point of view is it otherwise. Therefore when the game ends, it begins, that is it is complete and Self is at the beginning again. And so are You, but not the "you" you think you are; for that one the resistance game ends. For the You that transcends thoughts, hopes, beliefs, resistance, and all other non-You things, life has just begun at death of the mind, has always just begun, and is always complete and finished at the same time that it begins and is unfinished. For in that realm there is no resistance, there is no pain. Did you know that rocks are not in pain and do not resist the way things are?

I know you do not understand this. Neither do I and I *know* it, and so do you. In life "understanding" is the booby-prize. If you understood what I have just told you, all would be hopeless for you, for you would think you knew and in thinking you knew you would be doubly damned. Since you do not understand, you may have a chance for knowing and for knowing that you know.

Chapter Six:
Snake's Venom

What profits a man if he gains the whole world, and loses his own soul?

You may well ask, why struggle with these things? Why attempt to know what appears to be unknowable? Is it not enough to just subsist in life from day to day, to make sure that one is adequately fed, clothed, loved, and so forth? No, it is not. Your life depends on the degree of mastery you can attain in these matters. To the extent that you are unwilling to know, to the extent you are uncertain, you are dead. If you are unwilling to know anything, if you are completely uncertain, you will create a terminal illness or an accident and die. If you are willing to know only part of it, you will experience a degree of deadness. Your life *depends* on knowing about life—not understanding, but knowing.

A number of years ago an individual wrote a book, the purpose of which was to show the reader the techniques to be certain that he knew how to win in terms of success and to show also that one is truly responsible for the degree of success one is willing to have. The book was enormously successful. People read it in record numbers and found it to be of great value, that is, the book achieved its purposes. And while the book was enormously successful, it failed in one respect. While concentrating intently on success, the author lost sight of the qualities which make success worth having, without which money is worthless—worth "snake's venom" as the Iranians say, that is, less than nothing. That approach to satisfaction in life gets you through the gates to the game of life, but tells you nothing of the principles by which life itself is played. So, while being successful, you are winning a loser's game—the philosophy is not wrong, it is merely incomplete. *Winning Through Enlightenment* was written as a completion to the principles of success.

So, in the extreme, the purpose of entering this realm of human experience with me is to avoid physical death, that is doing away with yourself prematurely. In the less extreme, the purpose is completion, that is having a life that is fully satisfying for you and those around you. Someone once asked "What profits a man if he gains the whole world and loses his own soul?" So, suppose you gained all your mighty objectives? Without a Context or a Self to hold it in, you might as well die right now—worth snake's venom! Most of us are pursuing our objectives because we have no sense of Self, of Who We Are, hoping that the attainment of mighty goals will give us some clue about Who We Are and what we need to know about that is that quality and quantity exist in separate realms.

Chapter Seven:
Success

Have you not noticed that it is not enough to succeed?

In this chapter I want to outline the principles which allow you to achieve what this world terms "success." These principles are not difficult and will not take long to list, however you and I were taught directly and by example to "not know" these principles and to "believe" in other principles which lead to failure and make us righteous about our failure. So, although these are simple principles, you may have great barriers in your mind to living the truth of these principles.

For absolute simplicity I will list these numerically. You should look over these principles often due to the fact that you believe in that which does not work and because, if you are to truly make it in life, you must first succeed.

1.   Identify yourself as a contributor, that is one who, when she does what she does, contributes. Choose not to identify yourself as a survivor who might contribute someday, if you survive well enough. Being a survivor is worth snake's venom, that is less than nothing.

2.   Once you have identified yourself as a contributor to life, allow your contribution to survive you. If you are truly contributing, you will have the opportunity to become quite successful. Do not shun wealth under these circumstances.

You deserve it and you may have it without guilt or shame. Enjoy it. It validates your contribution.

3.   Constantly set goals, both short term and long term, and always do that which is necessary to achieve your goals. Never set a goal you are not willing to achieve, for then you can use that to invalidate yourself.

4.   Hold all failures as success; that is, each failure becomes an opportunity to propel you powerfully into your next success. If you become discouraged along the way, hold that as part of the process of winning the game.

5.   Always keep your agreements. Do not hold keeping your agreements as a worthy goal, simply keep them each and every time. Be trustworthy so that when you say a certain thing will be so, it is so. Always be where you say you will be, when you say you will be there. Always pay your debts when you say you will pay them.

6.   Never lie.

7.   Actively tell the truth.

8.   Hold others accountable in their relationship with you. Do not support anyone living by standards less than that to which they are committed. If they do, confront them, for your silence on the issue is support for them to live by low standards. Make sure others keep their agreements with you, for you are responsible for that as well.

9.   Empower others to succeed.

If you live by these principles, you will suceed. I promise it and I personally guarantee it. You will achieve not only enormous material wealth, you will achieve the admiration and respect of other people. And therein lies the danger, for when success comes your way you may think the game is over and retire. The game is not over and it never is—it is only complete. When something is complete it has only just begun. You are as far away from, and as close to, your purpose in life as you ever were. The game is over when you die and it is only apparently over then. Therefore there is one more principle:

10.   Recreate the game when your objectives are met. Keep playing. Never quit. Never retire. Retiring is worth snake's venom. The excitement in life is not in having achieved your goals, it is in setting them and striving for them. When you achieve your goals, set others immediately. Never rest on your laurels. Goals define the game so that you know when you have won, but winning is not the point. The point is playing the game.

That is basically it on success. Fairly simple stuff. No point in writing an entire book on it. That has already been done and I presume you can see that it is not enough. Have you not noticed that it is not enough to succeed? If not, perhaps you need to succeed in a big way so that you can fully experience that it is not quite enough. It is important to succeed, but that is only the beginning, a necessary beginning, but only a beginning.

Chapter Eight:
Empowered Self

The realization of yourself as empowered liberates you and completes success, which alone is inadequate.

Recently someone sent me a religious pamphlet quoting scriptural chapter and verse regarding the knowing of when one speaks with the authority of God and when one is speaking one's own mind. Apparently this was that person's response to reading *Winning Through Enlightenment*, and apparently came out of the perception of my writing as being put forth as the word of God. Nothing could be further from the truth. I do not see this material as coming from God, but on the other hand, it does not come out of my mind.

I want to reproduce some dictionary definitions for you here:

EMPOWER: 1. to give power or authority to; authorize; as, the president is empowered to veto legislation. 2. to give ability to; enable; permit as, science empowers men to control natural forces more effectively.

SELF: 1. the identity, character, or essential qualities of any person or thing...

Experience tells me that I must clearly define terms, if I am to be understood, and that I will still be misunderstood by those with minds which want to see everything in a predetermined fashion. So, please note: "Empower" means simply to give power or authority to and "Self" refers to the essential quality of a person.

Therefore Empowered Self is authorized to be effective in this world, and is your essential quality. In other words, it is Who You Are.

Self thinks creatively, Mind only reacts with recordings of thoughts. Self adds quality to life while Mind evaluates the quantities in life.

I presume that you can see that success (quantity) in life is not enough. If it were, you would have folded your cards and quit the game long ago, when you experienced your first success. As we discussed in the last chapter, the joy is in playing the game, not in succeeding with it, although the objective is to succeed. The question then becomes "How does one enable oneself to play a game, the objective of which is to succeed, and which yields pleasure as a function of playing rather than achieving the objective?" Clearly, who parents teach their children they (the children) are can not make it, can not win the game. Therefore, it is up to each of us to reach out to discover Who We Are and in that discovery, uncover for others the principles which make the world work.

Empowered Self has the following characteristics, that is You are characterized by the following:

1. No physicality; that is, not to be found in a particular place *and* found in all places equally, simultaneously.

2. Not bound to the confines of time, changeless in the face of constant, relentless change.

3. Not understandable, only creatable, essentially unprovable to Mind.

4. Non-judgemental, having no sense of "right" or "wrong."

5. Perfect in every way.

6. Having the power to forgive wrong-doing.

7. Having the power to create and destroy.

8. Willing to play the game of life by pretending that it is not

a game.

9.   Willing to create intrigue by hiding knowledge from itself; pretending not to know, thus making learning necessary.

10.   Loves others absolutely, perfectly, at all times and is willing to hide this to create intrigue.

11.   Oneness, that is there is only one Empowered Self, fully available to all, transcending space and time.

12.   The source of all knowledge.

The realization of yourself as empowered liberates you and completes success, which alone is inadequate.

Chapter Nine:
Liberation

You are now free. When you admit that is a choice you have.

So, the realization of yourself as empowered liberates you, but liberates you from what? It liberates you from who you think you are, who you were taught you are by yourself and others. It liberates you from habit patterns which you long since have accepted as part of yourself. It liberates you from believing in things as a matter of necessity and puts you at choice about your beliefs. It liberates you from the past and future and places you in present time. It liberates you from failure by recontextualizing failure to prepare you for the next breakthrough in life—in other words it tells the truth about failure. In a word, the realization of yourself as empowered transforms your experience of life, and once and for all you know that you are not who you thought you were.

However, there is an attachment to being that limited person you think you are and that attachment is righteousness. If you have spent your life saying you are green and someone hints that you might be blue, you will defend green practically to the death, even after you discover in your heart that you are blue. You do not want to make a lifetime of living like a green person seem worthless, a mistake, a miscalculation, unnecessary. If I told you that you love your father after you thought for years that you hated him, you would defend your position with great vigor, even after discovering that you loved him. If I told you that you were extremely intelligent and you had spent your life proving otherwise, you would not quickly give up your position and make being unintelligent wrong.

Who you think you are, that is a limited self, is tenacious and wants above all things to be right, especially about its image of itself. So, I know you will not give up easily, and I know that eventually you will give up, because the truth once said has awesome power to transform. Someone once said, "You shall know the truth, and the truth shall set you free." What someone did not say is that the truth will anger you, nor did someone say when you would be set free, once having known the truth. What does happen is that a process begins which will set you free. When that process is finished will be a function of your intention.

Really, though, it does not matter when you are liberated or transformed, for you are already transformed. Thinking of yourself as a limited self and acting accordingly is merely a game Self plays for amusement. Deep in your heart of hearts, you know it. When you admit it is up to you.

BOOK II:
THE INTEGRITY STATES

Integrity is the condition of being whole, lacking no component parts. One is born with integrity into a world which has little integrity. To survive in such a world one must give up, at least for a time, one's natural integrity. To regain your integrity is to regain your Self and is the expression of transformation.

Your integrity state profoundly alters both your circumstances and your experience of your circumstances.

Empower Source
Abundance
Normal
↳Emergency
  ↳Danger
    ↳Non-existence
      ↳Injury
        ↳Uncertainty
          Opposition
          Disloyalty

Chapter One:
The Fall From Grace

The fall from grace is inevitable. So the question is: "Will you rise again?"

It is not natural to be unhappy. Being less than full of joy is a mind condition you adopted when you were quite young in order to get your way with others. If you will go to a newborn nursery (at your nearest hospital) and peer through the window at newborn infants, you will notice that when a newborn is not in physical pain (hungry, cold, etc.), the expression the newborn will give you is joy, enthusiasm, interest and curiosity. This state is called Normal, to remind you of your natural state before you created negative emotions to manipulate others. You were born into Normal.

Given that you live in the world that you live in, there is a problem with existing in your natural state (Normal) and that difficulty is that no one notices you, or if they do notice, they think you are abnormal. Just try being full of joy, enthusiasm, interest and curiosity on the street or on the bus. If you really express that fully, you will be locked up! At the very least, no one will speak to you. You think you cannot get your way while being in Normal and when you are an infant, dependent on others for your basic needs, this is a real problem. When an infant is deprived of those basic things needed for life—air, food, and affection—what we see is a descent into the next lower integrity state, Emergency.

In Emergency we see crying, spitting, etc. designed to induce adults to administer basic needs. This is the first hint of "unhappiness" in a human being *and reveals the basic nature of unhap-*

31

piness: to manipulate others. Most human emotions then have this purpose: to persuade others to deliver. In the beginning of life that which the infant wants delivered is basic to life itself. However this is not so later in life. As an infant, Emergency works so well that the infant learns that all he need do to get practically anything he wants is to act unhappy. In the beginning this is clearly an Act, but as the years pass the Act is practiced so many times that the actor or actress begins to experience it as real. The emotions take hold of Who the actor is—Empowered Self falls from grace and Who You Are is disempowered in order to manipulate others and get what your mind wants.

As a few years pass, and the Act, or Mind, begins to take hold of the Self, the Self forgets its state of natural grace, or enlightenment. When the Act becomes real to the actor or actress it is called Danger. Gone is the playful lightness of the Emergency state, the game is now serious, that is it seems real. The emotions experienced are fear, dread and anxiety. One is no longer the author of life, but a character in the play. In Danger, the child is like a person drowning who can see life slipping away, but who still sees hope of saving himself. Given that children are considered less than human in our society, the fall into Danger, and usually lower, is practically inevitable. So, the question is: will you rise again?

When hope disappears the child sinks into a state called Nonexistence. In the U.S. the dominant deprivation children experience is the absence of affection—expression of love. In some other cultures the dominant deprivation is starvation. In either case the coping response is the same. Non-existence is a state in which you do not experience yourself as fully connected with your environment or the people in it. You feel distant, separated, unimportant. It ceases to matter to you that you are not nurtured and it ceases to matter to you if others are nurtured. Non-existence prepares you for the next step down, Injury. It is the border line condition below which lie the four states of No Responsibility.

In Injury we see the advent of self-destructive behavior disguised as mistakes and accidents. The disguise is so complete that it deceives even the person in Injury. I term this integrity state Injury, because it is in this state that bodily injury is likely to occur. You should not ride in a car driven by a person in Injury. In children we see skinned knees, broken bones, and sometimes "accidental" death. Recently a child in this integrity state rode her bicycle directly in front of my car without looking. Fortunately, I was driving very slowly and was able to stop in the nick of time. Often the mistakes people make while in Injury harm others but the redeeming feature of Injury is that you can count on the person to clean up the damage caused. There is still a sense of responsibility in the person so that others are not blamed for the mistakes made. So, you can count on a person in Injury to repair the damage done. On the other hand, you can also count on the person to do more damage. Children in Injury typically receive a lot of criticism which tends to drive them into the next lower state of integrity, Uncertainty.

The password into Uncertainty is "I don't know." The dominant experience to almost every situation is that of "not knowing." When you are uncertain you are not only withdrawn and distant, but you are wondering if you have any responsibility for your life whatsoever. It is the last way-station before a dramatic fall into a state if integrity from which it is very hard to recover. Most people have reached Uncertainty by age twelve years, and with the onset of adolescence are ready for the plunge into Opposition and Disloyality.

THE READING IS DIFFICULT FROM HERE TO PAGE 58 DUE TO THE NATURE OF THE INFORMATION. PERSIST UNTIL THEN AND EVERYTHING WILL LIGHTEN UP.

Empower Source
Abundance
Normal
Emergency
Danger
Non-existence
Injury
Uncertainty
↳ Opposition
↳ Disloyalty

Chapter Two:
Hitting the Bottom

You will descend into Disloyalty by age 20. At that point you can start proving there is nothing else, or your can turn your life around.

The two states, Opposition and Disloyalty, could be said to be a box, from which it is very difficult to escape, the instructions for escaping being printed on the *outside* of the box. In these two states, not only have you given up being cause in the matter of your own integrity, you also have the remnant of Uncertainty—you say "I don't know" a lot. Or, sometimes, as a defense against "not knowing," you will become a "know-it-all."

Most people are down to Opposition by the time they are teenagers. In Opposition you do not have a sense of your own self-worth and what you want to do about it is to try to prove that no one else is worthy either. The technique for doing this is to oppose everyone around you. You do not have any solutions for problems, you only have criticism of the problems themselves. The characteristic which distinguishes Opposition from the next step down, Disloyalty, is that in Opposition, your status as an enemy to life is clearly stated. Everyone knows where you stand because you tell them in no uncertain terms.

In Disloyalty you pretend to be supportive of others while you are scheming to oppose them. You take a private glee is seeing someone fail and you are yourself a failure. People in Disloyalty take a certain pleasure in reading the headlines of the daily newspaper because they can count on a story about personal or societal failure.

In Opposition and Disloyalty you are essentially powerless. You may gather a lot of force and be able to dominate others with your force, but as far as making any kind of powerful contribution to a higher quality of life, you can forget it. Also, you can count on experiencing a lot of negative emotions within your own private experience. And this will be manifested to the world by your willingness to do anything to decrease the aliveness of others. You conceive of yourself as "victim" and others as persecutors. And your solution is to do everything you can to victimize others, never quite seeing that you are the one who pays the price. In the extreme, suicide and murder occur in these states of integrity. The other solution to the viewpoint that people are "victims" is to try to save them in a way that truly disempowers them. Certain religious movements fall into this activity. Religion, through the ages, has fallen down the scale through all the states of integrity, even though the creators of the various faiths existed in an integrity state higher than Normal (Empower Source—which we will discuss later).

If you are wondering where you fit on the integrity scale, you can be fairly certain that you either fit into Uncertainty or below or that you have been there in your life and are somewhere on your way up the ladder. About 80% of humanity exists in Disloyalty at any given time. For purposes of reading this book, assume that you are in Disloyalty, and I will illuminate the instructions for moving out of the box. Remember that the instructions for getting out of the box are printed on the *outside* of the box. So, these instructions will seem "wrong" to you if you are inside the box and they will be very difficult for you to see. Also, I will present you with the manner in which you can move up from whatever position on the integrity scale in which you find yourself. Once you deliver your Self from the box you will automatically move up the integrity scale as the years of your life pass, the only question being "How fast will you move up?" Our purpose here will be to present you with the principles which allow you to move up at your maximum rate.

This then is the path for most individuals. The fall from grace or enlightenment into which you were born has usually reached Opposition by mid-adolescence and Disloyalty by the early 20s.

Life then becomes about proving that there is nothing else (no outside of the box) or about escaping to the outside of the box into Responsibility (Non-existence and above). Said another way, the game of life becomes about being either right *or* passing out of the realm of Effect and into being Cause in the matter of your own life and your own integrity. It is the struggle to regain your lost humanity. This book is about that game: Transformation.

Empower Source
Abundance
Normal
Emergency
Danger
Non-existence
Injury
Uncertainty
Opposition
↳Disloyalty

Chapter Three:
The Escape from Disloyalty

*The instructions for escape from the box of
Disloyalty are printed on the outside of the box. If
you will listen, I will read you the instructions.*

Disloyalty is the lowest integrity state. It is that integrity state in which people lie, cheat, steal, betray, take revenge, are jealous, dislike, hate, conspire against others, resent, feel depressed, blame, covet, and I could go on and on. What, you may ask, is the meaning of all this? Obviously this sort of existence is not worth living and that is exactly what a person in Disloyalty thinks: "A life like this is not worth living." Occasionally a person in Disloyalty puts an end to life, their own or others. More often people who are in this integrity state cannot face, or tell the truth about their condition, so they simply lie or pretend that they are in a different integrity state.

So, *pretense* is the name of the game in Disloyalty. Since the instructions for getting out of the box of Disloyalty are printed on the outside of the box, a person in the box (given that he cannot tell the truth) simply pretends to be on the outside of the box. Therefore, when you deal with people in Disloyalty, they may appear to be in a higher integrity state. They are keeping their agreements, for example, because they feel obligated, not because they simply keep their agreements. They say nice things to you because they are supposed to do that, not because they experience you in complimentary terms. They are the people who may say the "right" things at the "right" times, but you know in your heart that you should not turn your back on them or trust them in any way. However they are often so convincing that you forget to trust your experience of them and you pay the price, for they cannot be trusted. When you trust such a person and it occurs to that person that it would be in their immediate interest to betray your trust, your trust *will* be betrayed, you can count on it. You will think you are supported one minute and in the next instant the rug will be pulled out from under you and you will have been betrayed. Sometimes the disloyal person will betray you for no other reason than to stay in the practice of betraying people. So, a seemingly capricious betrayal or withdrawal of support is the rule of the day in Disloyalty.

A person in Disloyalty is intensely unhappy. Depression, anger, a pervasive sense of worthlessness is the grist of life for the disloyal person. But remember that they are great pretenders. If you are in Disloyalty, you are unlikely to admit it even to yourself because part of the pretense is toward yourself. Your only clue may be general unhappiness. If you are dealing with a person in Disloyalty, you must be willing to trust your experience of the other person if you expect to protect yourself from treachery. Trusting your experience is vastly different from trusting your concepts. When you trust your concepts you look at the evidence and ignore what you know intuitively. If you are in Disloyalty yourself, you will not be able to trust your experience of others since you lost touch with that long ago. When you meet up with other people in Disloyalty, you have practically no protection. The classic example of this is the employer in Disloyalty interviewing another person in Disloyalty for a job and making the judgement based on the resume rather than experience: screwed every time! And wonders why his business does not work!

I want to emphasize the skill with which a smart person in Disloyalty can disguise his integrity state. The ultimate example is that of the criminal who plans the "perfect" crime, that is the crime which is not even known to have occurred. There *is* such a thing as a perfect crime, by the way. You only hear about the imperfect ones.

HOW TO MOVE UP AND OUT OF DISLOYALTY

Few people in Disloyalty are interested in the rules for getting out of Disloyalty, since such people are busy pretending they are not in Disloyalty in the first place. Therefore, to show interest in how to move up, even if that interest is revealed only to oneself, would be to admit the pretense and give up the Act. So, if you are unhappy and you are wanting to put this book down right now, I am talking to you, especially you. For you see, to get out of the box of Disloyalty, you first must tell the truth about being in it. Remember all these instructions are printed on the *outside* of the box and will not make sense to you if you are inside the box. Also, a disloyal person would rather die than tell the truth about anything, including that he would rather die than tell the truth about anything. So, it will require an act of great courage to tell the truth about your disloyalty. But you must tell it, to yourself and others. We need to know that you know that you cannot be trusted. We all already know that you cannot be trusted, we simply do not know that you know. We think you are still pretending. So, if you want out of Disloyalty, you must tell the truth about yourself. *There is no other way.* You cannot be any bigger than you are willing to be small.

And it requires great courage, because the state you will move into will not be much higher (Opposition) and, in fact, you will make a lot of open enemies when you move up. But, at least you will be open about it, which will give them an opportunity to be open about it. Remember, nothing changes, nothing disappears until you tell the absolute truth about it.

After you have told the truth about the fact of your disloyalty, you must choose to trust yourself. At the same times that you admit that you cannot be trusted, you must choose to trust yourself. Obviously you choose to trust yourself without any evidence that you can be trusted. You see, trustability is *not* something that happens after you have proven yourself, proof manifests *after* you choose to trust yourself. Choosing, in this instance, is synonymous with creating. You simply create yourself as trustworthy and then you have opportunities to practice your trustworthiness.

As you move out of Disloyalty you are moving away from the realm of Effect, that is you are moving away from blaming others for the way your life and your experience of your life is turning out. You are by no means *out* of the realm of Effect, you have simply moved in the direction of the experience of Cause, that is being the author of life, rather than a character in the play. The next step up is Opposition and you are still in a box. Too bad. You have only begun your journey upward, a journey which may require years. Have heart, the trip is worth it.

Empower Source
Abundance
Normal
Emergency
Danger
Non-existence
Injury
Uncertainty
⌁Opposition
Disloyalty

Chapter Four:
The Escape From Opposition

To move up from Opposition you have to give up being "right" about your beliefs. Therefore, you may never make it.

When your dominant choice is to trust yourself, you will find that where you live your life from is Opposition. You will make frequent forays into Disloyalty, and also into higher integrity states, but your dominant mode of expressing Empowered Self will be by opposing who and what is around you, you will live your life *from Opposition*.

In Opposition you are basically arguing with the way it is. If you sat down and thought for a century to come up with a formula to produce turmoil and unhappiness in your relationships with others, Opposition would be the crowning achievement of all those years of thinking. In Disloyalty you were in opposition to life, however you lied and said that you were not, and you acted (pretended) as if you were not in opposition. When you are in the state of integrity called Opposition you are still lying about it (saying you are not in Opposition), but you no longer pretend, rather you openly oppose your relationships working and you oppose results being achieved in your personal life and business life, and in the personal and business lives of others. You are no longer covert. To yourself you are saying, "This is the way to get results: I have to oppose all these people because they are all wrong in the way they are approaching life." Furthermore you say, "I have the right answers and my job is to make them see how right I am and how wrong they are. If they will only play by my rules, everything will

41

turn out." However, if you actually force someone to play by your rules, nothing works because life working is not a function of the rules in the first place. But, what you say about it is that the rules are at fault and then you arbitrarily make up more, better or different rules and try to impose them on others. Many marriages go through this sequence for years and years. One or both partners are looking for the "right" rules to follow, thinking that the rules will make the relationship work, never quite realizing that Who You Are, Self, and your willingness to express Self in a high state of integrity, allows the relationship to work.

So the more you stick to the rules in life, the less life works. The inflexibility of a person stuck with the rules is a classic in an organization that is going under and in a relationship which is not working. When a business goes under, it is difficult to pretend, because the salaries cannot be paid. However, when a relationship goes under, it is easy to pretend, so if you operate your marriage or relationship from Opposition (and most people do) and it does not work, that is, it is not satisfying (and it never is), then you can choose to go into Disloyalty and pretend it *is* working. I refer to a relationship in this condition as Dead or in the state of Death. Oddly enough the way out is not to find a new relationship, but to have the courage to move up the integrity scale instead of down. Unfortunately what is just above Disloyalty and Death in relationships is Opposition and you already tried that, so that does not appear to be the way out. Remember you are in a box, the instructions to escape from which are not obvious, that is they are printed on the outside of the box. This is true in Opposition also. Mostly what people do after Opposition (with its rules) has failed is to sink into Disloyalty and either die in the relationship or separate and look for a new relationship. Unfortunately for you, if you try this, you will take your integrity state into the next relationship.

So, it is difficult to move back into Opposition after months or years of being in Opposition and hating it and not knowing how to move to a higher state of integrity. It takes real courage to return to something that is higher which has the appearance of being lower. When you are in the Disloyalty/Opposition Box, you cannot distinguish up from down, and you do not trust others to tell you which is which. You typically defend yourself by thinking you know it all and that unhappiness and suffering is just the way life is. You probably think people who appear happy are faking it, since when you appear happy, you *are* faking it (pretense). People who are enthusiastically happy, obviously not faking it, arouse extreme hate and opposition in you which you hide and pretend is not there. You simply do not know what real happiness, satisfaction, and enthusiasm are about.

If you are willing to admit to being in Opposition, you have already taken the first step to rising into the next higher state of integrity. In addition to telling the truth, which is a requirement to make anything disappear in life, you must then look and see the results Opposition is getting in your life and tell the truth about that. The results are costly and almost always they are the results you do not want, but which make you right, and being right is your payoff. Then to propel yourself into the next higher state (Uncertainty) you must choose to go for the results you want, rather than the results which make you right. Invariably you will find that you cannot play by your old "rules" if you are to get the desired results. You will have to be "wrong" about having had those rules and create new rules. The first and foremost rule is the following: *There are no rules.* Once you realize that there are no "right" rules for living life, you can create the rules which allow you to adapt to the conditions you find yourself in right now.

So when you choose to go for the results you want in life you will be moving up the integrity scale to Uncertainty, which is no bowl of cherries, but it is a noticeable improvement from Opposition. The most difficult move to make in the entire integrity scale is from Opposition to Uncertainty, because you have to give up being "right" about what you think about life. You become, in a word, uncertain.

Empower Source
Abundance
Normal
Emergency
Danger
Non-existence
Injury
Uncertainty
Opposition
Disloyalty

Chapter Five: Uncertainty

To move up from Uncertainty, you must be willing to create your direction in life, for no reason other than pure choice.

In Disloyalty and Opposition you truly did not know up from down on the integrity scale; you had no idea of what made life work when it did and what made life not work when it did not work. And you were doubly damned because you thought you knew, you were sure you knew, and you made up beliefs and rules to prove to yourself and others that you knew. So, when situations arose in life which were difficult to deal with, you consulted your list of sayings and platitudes and you gave yourself advice or you gave your friends advice, thinking of yourself as full of wisdom. When your advice did not work, you looked for new rules, new platitudes to believe in and said "Aha! Life hasn't been working because I have the wrong posters on my wall!" And you replaced those posters with different posters, or perhaps you simply added more posters or different posters with different platitudes, rules, or beliefs. Perhaps you changed the person you listen to for advice or you quit going to church or you started going to church or you found some unusual cult to give you answers. Any change would serve to camouflage from yourself the fact that the believing process itself was at fault.

Most of us live out our entire lives searching for the rules to make life work, thus staying in Disloyalty and Opposition. We are seekers looking for a saviour. In this condition you are likely to try anything, including drugs, to alter your experience. By the way, this is where the drug culture exists: in Disloyalty and Opposition, looking for answers. Supposedly the mind alteration of a drug is the "answer." But religion can also fit neatly into this category. If you use religion as "the answer" in life, *thus avoiding being the answer yourself*, you might as well be on drugs as your answer. Also, you may look to psychology, psychiatry, or psychoanalysis for the answer and you might as well be on drugs if you think THE TRUTH is to be found in these disciplines. I am *not* saying that drugs, religion and psychological endeavors are not valuable; they *are* valuable, to the exact degree that you take responsibility for adding the value. But the truth is ineffable, unspeakable, and therefore cannot be taught in concepts.

If you move up from Opposition by giving up being right about your rules, you will find yourself in Uncertainty. You will be certain of only one thing: you will know that you do not know. And you will know that no one else knows. You will be *willing* to not know, to take down the platitudes from your wall or in your mind and just hang out with the possibility that you have no idea of what works and what does not work and furthermore that those gurus you thought had the answers do not have the answer either, that in fact there may not be an "answer." In a word you will "not know." You will say "I don't know" a lot in conversations which come up about life. You will simply listen to others who think they know and support them in expressing themselves, knowing that they do not know either, only think they know. You will not be telling them you know they do not know, since that will not serve them. You simply let them express themselves. When you are certain that you are uncertain, *when you know that you do not know, you are out of the box of Disloyalty/Opposition.*

You are still in the realm of Effect, that is you are not yet creating your experience by free choice, however, you can see for the first time that there might be such a thing as creativity for you. I mean that it might be possible for you to be truly creative—not that stuff I would term "inventively manipulative" which is attached to a lot of pride and arrogance. I am referring here to true creativity, the sort of creativity which is continuous and flowing—creation of your experience. This is contrasted with the experience of the realm of Effect where you are essentially a reaction machine, that is you have a store of responses, emotional and behavioral, and you simply play out those responses when situations arise in life. You have an anger response, a jealousy response, a depression response, etc. At Uncertainty you are still a reaction device, but you are beginning to have some appreciation of that fact, and you are beginning to sense what liberty might be.

Nevertheless, when you are in Uncertainty, at the same time you know that you do not know, you will be hoping that someone knows and you will be on the lookout for that person. You will be susceptible to becoming a follower and you will be looking for the prince or princess to come and have a relationship with you, load you up on the white horse or put you in the pumpkin carriage and take you away to where serenity is, to where the answers will be given to you. If you actually attach yourself to someone for this purpose, you are right back into Disloyalty and you will have to go through Opposition to the prince or princess to regain Uncertainty. You cannot have a successful relationship in Uncertainty or below.

To move up from Uncertainty, where you can have a working relationship, you must be willing to choose a course in life, not because it is "right" and not because someone told you to choose it (a guru), but simply because you choose it. This kind of choice is the first act of responsibility on your way up the scale of integrity. For example, you may choose an occupation, but you choose it because you choose it, not because it is the "right" one, but simply because you choose it, realizing that you are the source of satisfaction and your job is not. I am amazed at people who spend their entire lives looking for the "right" job and are not willing to make the job they have "right." So, to move up from Uncertainty you *choose*, just as a life principle you *choose*. You choose what? You choose what is, naturally. Simply take a look at what there is in your life and choose it. If you are unhappy with what is in your life, you forgot to choose it. It is not that it brought unhappiness with it (you added that), you simply forgot to choose what you chose—that is you did choose it, you simply forgot to be responsible for your choice. So, if you have a certain relationship in your life, perhaps someone that at one time you thought was the prince or princess, and who does not look so good to you any more, here is what happened. One morning you woke up and you forgot to choose that person. You said "How on earth did I get stuck with this?" and from that time on you began to make up faults on which to concentrate. You forgot to choose that person to be the way they are. Or, perhaps the same process has happened with your job. You forgot to choose the job you have one morning and that very day it began to look like the "wrong" job. You may even have forgotten to choose yourself, that is the individual person, position, carbon-based unit, body—however you want to say it—you may have forgotten to choose to be the person you are for now. In that case *all* your circumstances in life will look like the wrong circumstances because you are the wrong person. Ever look in the mirror and wonder "Is that really me?"

So, when you move up from Uncertainty, you choose what is, *all* of what is, that is you realize the natural perfection of what actually exists. You will then move into Injury, the first state in which you can be trusted and the first state in which you can have a satisfying relationship. You are still not at the level of Cause, but you are closing in on it. When you get to Uncertainty it takes courage to move up to Injury because you *will* injure yourself, and even when you are in Uncertainty, you know what the next step holds, you know it intuitively and this will tend to stick you with being in Uncertainty, the "I don't know" stage of life.

Chapter Six:
Injury

*To move up the scale from Injury, here is what
you must do: serve others, give freely of yourself,
even when you are sure you are a sucker to do so.*

My observation is that at least 80% of the people in this world
live their lives out of Disloyalty. Most have experienced Uncertainty at some time or another, but few people live their lives from
above Opposition. I do not mean to imply that people have not experienced some of the higher states of integrity, I am merely referring to the position from which you live your life, or to put in
another way, the level of integrity you come from in your experience of life. So, almost everyone can relate to the description of
Disloyalty and Opposition and most have some sense of Uncertainty, but very few are able to relate to the descriptions of higher
states of integrity.

A characteristic of the integrity scale is that a description of the
states of integrity at or below where you live your life now sounds
familiar and a description of higher states sounds very unfamiliar,
somewhat unreal. You might say that you can see *down* the integrity scale, but you cannot see *up* into states higher than your own.
Therefore, as the descriptions ascend beyond your personal experience you will tend not to believe that people can exist in these
states. You will think that I am lying to you. For example, if I told
you that there is an integrity state in which unhappiness is never experienced, you might think of that as pure bologna. Yet, the truth is
that there is not only an integrity state where unhappiness is never

experienced, there are even higher states than that.

As we enter Injury we are at the last way-station before entering into the realm of Cause. You are still not creating your experience of life, but at least you are willing to be responsible for your experience. In other words, at this level you give up blaming others. When you choose and move up out of Uncertainty, what you choose is what is, not what you wish would be, but what actually is. You choose it to be the way it is and this is the first hint from you that you may be seeing that you created, and are responsible for, your experience of the way it is.

In the lower integrity states you make a lot of mistakes in life and in Injury you continue to make a lot of mistakes. The difference is that you no longer blame conditions and other people and you can be trusted to repair your mistakes. On the other hand, you can also be trusted to make further needless mistakes. This then is a double-edged sword. People know you will mess up in life and this drives them away, but they also see that you do not blame them *and* you repair your mistakes, so they are also drawn to you. At this stage of going up the integrity scale, you will notice that you are invited to social functions, you are fully included, others begin to think of you and include you in their plans. This is the lowest state of integrity in which you can have satisfying successful relationships.

As I said before, you are still in the realm of Effect, you are still a "victim" in life, but you can begin to appreciate that you might be the source of your troubles. You cannot see it clearly yet, it is only an intuition, a suspicion, something you are willing to consider, perhaps even believe, it sounds "reasonable." And yet it is not an experience at this stage. You may spend months or years at this level of integrity, knowing that you are able to move up and simply wondering when. And, you *will* injure yourself, physically, emotionally, and all needlessly. Also, you will injure others in these ways. But always, you clean up the damage and this truly sets you apart from 80% of people in the world.

In order to move up you are already doing one of the things you must do: you are repairing the damage you do. The other thing you must do is not so obvious, so I will simply tell you outright: you must serve others. This will be your biggest, most powerful barrier to moving out of Injury, out of Effect and "victim"—you will resist serving others for a complex set of beliefs which are very common in this world. Not only must you serve others, you must serve someone who is out of the realm of Effect, someone who knows Who she/he is, someone who knows himself or herself as an embodiment of Self. There is no movement up the scale in serving another person in Effect. Not only that, you must serve this person in the context of a purpose mightier than yourself and mightier than the relationship you have with the person you serve. Most marital relationships which are otherwise successful bog down exactly here: they have no purpose larger than the relationship itself and they are not designed to serve anyone who exists out of the realm of Effect. Therefore, the relationship has no larger purpose than itself and it invariably turns in on itself and consumes itself in petty, small, insignificance: issues that not only do not matter, but are not real, that is they are made up out of the boredom of non-service.

As I said, this issue of service will be your largest barrier to moving out of the realm of Effect. By far the great majority of human beings never make it because they are afraid of being conned. That is what I said: afraid of being conned. You are afraid you will be tricked into doing a service for someone and there will be no payoff for you, so you quietly, carefully evaluate every opportunity to serve to see what is in it for you and you never quite realize that this paranoid fear of being tricked into serving is your only barrier to moving out of the "victim" position in life and becoming truly creative. If you are to get past this one, you will have to serve a person and a purpose in the condition of being sure you *are* being conned. There is no other way. You must give of your Self freely even while you see your Self as a limited, easily conned, little self. Too bad! You will get over it if you keep serving. When you do you will pass through an ephemeral zone of experience called Non-existence which is a distressing transition from Effect into Cause.

Empower Source
        Abundance
Normal
        Emergency
        Danger
        ⌐ Non-existence
                Injury
                Uncertainty
                        Opposition
                        Disloyalty

Chapter Seven:
Non-existence

Breakthrough often occurs after breakdown.

In all the states of integrity below Non-existence you literally exist as a function of conditions and circumstances. If those conditions and circumstances were to change drastically, you would not have a sense of your own identity in the world. You thought you were your skin color, your social and economic class, your education, your "tastes." You have probably existed even as a function of the clothes you wore and the people you knew. So you existed as a function of everything else. It seemed to you that if all that disappeared, you might also disappear, at least "you" as you thought of yourself might cease to be, to "die" or cease to exist. In fact, during events like the stock market crash of 1929 when many of those "things" did disappear for some people, a not uncommon solution was suicide. Those people were thrown prematurely into the state of Non-existence. I say prematurely because they did not choose it but were literally thrown into it by a turn of economic events. The man who thought of himself as a business tycoon suddenly did not know who he was when his business tycoon circumstances were destroyed. So, he lept out the 10th story window not really regretting his own death since, for him, he had ceased to exist anyway; he existed in a new and totally foreign state called Non-existence.

Above Non-existence on the integrity scale is the realm of Cause where your existence is not dependent on the conditions of your life but rather is created by you from moment to moment from nothing. That does not mean that there are no conditions in your life, it merely means that your experience of your Self is not constructed out of things, circumstances, and conditions. It does not depend on your money, your clothes, your body, your friends, or any "thing" else, but is created by you on no evidence. In the realm of Cause or Source (synonymous) you cannot show proof of Who You Are when you create your Self. It is a pure creation out of which proof flows as time passes. If proof does not flow after the creation, there was no creation but merely one more tricky manifestation of the pretense of Disloyalty—you lied again.

So, that which is below Non-existence is easy to describe and that which is above Non-existence is easy to describe, but Non-existence, by its very nature is described in terms of not being what is above and below on the integrity scale. Nonexistence then is only describable as what it is not, not what it is. Below Non-existence you are attached to life, but as a victim. Above Non-existence you are attached to life, but as a creator. In Non-existence you are not attached to life. You are not dis*contented*, since that is a function of being a victim at effect, in fact you are contented but you feel distant, separated, unimportant.

Non-existence is a gray zone between Effect and Cause, between victim and creator, and it is very difficult to stay in this transition zone. You will tend to move up into Cause or back down into Effect very quickly because in Non-existence you have no sense of personal identity. At least as a victim you have a false identity and as a creator you have your real identity, but in Non-existence, you have neither.

Therefore, if you are playing the integrity game with me, you will want to know how to move up the scale, and as usual there is a technique for this. As you touch on the realm of Cause, for the first time you will see that your life might be of genuine consequence to the world, that you might make a contribution that would mean something to the quality of life on earth. While you were in Effect, you did not dare dream this except in the pretense of Disloyalty where you knew your dreams had no hope of success. Moving into Cause you realize that your dream of being effective in the world is not just a dream. The glamour and pride melt away and you begin to see that you can create any role for your Self that you choose. Therefore to move out of Non-existence you simply make a goal and start being appropriate to your goal. Being appropriate to your goal means simply looking to see how things are actually accomplished in the world and then going for the accomplishments of your choice. To do this you must transcend your beliefs about the way you think things are accomplished and see how things *really* work. In other words you give up being "right" about the way things "should" be. Simply stated, you look and see what is needed and wanted, then you enroll others to participate in supplying what is needed and wanted. The key to enrolling people is communication—if you do not communicate, you cannot enroll. So to move out of Non-existence you choose a project and you communicate and enroll other people in your project, your "game" in life. For example: one of my projects is writing books and having people read them and create miracles from reading them. Since you are reading this you have evidence that I communicated and enrolled you in reading this. I may have done this directly or I may have communicated and enrolled others to communicate and enroll others, and so on, until you finally read this book. The point is that one's contribution makes no difference until one communicates and enrolls others. You must come out of hiding and make your Self known. Your days of anonymity are numbered.

When you move up the integrity scale you will encounter a sense of risk and danger—you are no longer snugly safe, you stand a good chance of failing. But remember, you cannot win until you are willing to risk failing. So, as you move up into the integrity state known as Danger, welcome the risk of failure as a necessary stage on the way up to being Cause, to power, contribution and creativity. You are regaining your lost grace—welcome a little risk, welcome a *lot* of risk, and welcome failure if that comes. Who You Are is infinitely larger than any failure and all your failures are merely object lessons in reality anyway. They prepare you for the next breakthrough in life. If that were not the truth I would not say it to you! Breakthrough often comes after breakdown.

Empower Source
Abundance
Normal
Emergency
⤶ Danger
Non-existence
Injury
Uncertainty
Opposition
Disloyalty

Chapter Eight:
Danger

The danger is that you may fail.

As you move up from Non-existence, you will have a pro-ject—a form with which to express yourself in a transformed and transforming way, a method to improve the quality of life, to bind you to empowering others as the only way to become powerful yourself. You may choose to make this the work which yields your income or you may elect to simply volunteer your time and create your project as a gift to transformation in our world. Either way, you will immediately encounter the integrity state called Danger. Danger is a land of adventure, and real danger. The danger is that you may fail. In fact, you will certainly experience some failures along the way. You will set inappropriate goals, you will not meet your goals, you will find yourself using unethical means to achieve your ends, you will discover that your project will not support itself financially, and I could go on with a very long list with which I am intimately familiar. But through all this the adventure of it all prevails. After all, it is *your* project. You own it. You would die for it, not to mention risk all you own. So, the danger involved is seen as an exciting and necessary part of the game. The wonderment and the anxiety are welcomed. You are curious to see what the future holds. Problems are experienced as those situations which lure you on to new discovery.

To move up the integrity scale from Danger to the next level (Emergency) you must eliminate unethical attitudes and behavior and recognize those areas in which you sabotage yourself, and correct them. When you do, your project will attract enormous attention and the frenetic activity you attract around you will remind you of an emergency room. Your project will be almost too hot to handle.

Empower Source
Abundance
Normal
⤶ Emergency
Danger
Non-existence
Injury
Uncertainty
Opposition
Disloyalty

Chapter Nine:
Emergency

*To move into the frenetic state of Emergency,
simply see all your failures as perfect object lessons
to discover reality.*

To move from Danger to Emergency, you must be willing to
hold all your failures as object lessons in discovering the way life is,
the way things work, in short, how to make your project representative of your Self, Empowered Self.

The activity you experience in Emergency is frenetic and
urgent, as it is difficult to complete your goals on a day-to-day
basis. Nevertheless, there is a prevailing feeling of strong interest in
the project and an attitude of certainty and satisfaction. Problems
are seen as challenges and the solutions are seen in the context of
cooperation. To put it in another way, the perception of opposition
begins to disappear and cooperation becomes the order of the day.
At this level you can recognize that all of what you thought was opposition in the past was merely reaction to your own disloyal actions, lessons in reality and ultimately the perfect lessons you needed at that time. The villians in life begin to disappear from your experience. In fact, they were never there. There was only you.

To move up from Emergency, it is important to promote your
project. the essence of promotion is communication and enroll-
ment. Let people know about what you are up to, enlist their alignment in your purpose and your project, allow them to contribute,
to make it their project. So, you begin to give away your project
so that it belongs to everyone in such a way that each recipient can

give it away so that it belongs to whoever receives it.

You must then further stiffen your integrity and prepare for expanded activity for you are soon to move into Normal, the state of integrity into which you were born. The difference, of course, being that you were not born with a project to express your normality.

Empower Source
⤷Abundance
Normal
Emergency
Danger
Non-existence
Injury
Uncertainty
Opposition
Disloyalty

Chapter Ten:
Normal

In Normal you are back where you started with an opportunity to move even higher.

In the Integrity state called Normal, your project flourishes naturally, without effort. It serves its purpose, it pays its own way, it doesn't require promotion to hold its own, it is truly self-perpetuating. If you quit promoting and expanding it, it would not disappear, it would at least stay at the same level if not expand. Your emotional state reflects enthusiasm and your attitude is one of admiration for people—all people. Problems are recognized as opportunities and you are enhanced by solving them.

To move above Normal is a leap of great faith since you were born into Normal and have never known a higher integrity state. The leap above Normal ordinarily comes as a result of your relationship with someone who has made it to the higher integrity states. If you can look at that person and see that he or she is a few notches above you in the area of integrity, then you can consciously learn from that person the methods for moving up. Up to and including Normal, your integrity was consumed in handling your individuality in a responsible manner. When you move above Normal, your integrity becomes intimately linked to the integrity of other people. Life becomes a you *and* me proposition rather than a me proposition.

The next level up is Abundance. In Abundance, life is abundant not only for you and your project, but it is abundant for others and they want to play in your project and expand it. This effect is magnified as you move into the highest integrity state: Empower Source.

There is an old Zen saying "When I know who you are, I serve you, When I know who I am, I am you." The truth of this becomes apparent as you move above Normal.

To move up from Normal, ask yourself the question: "How can I empower and enable the people I am in relationship with?" Answer the question and be true to the answer. Be willing to forget yourself as an individual and *become* your community, your organization, your world. Don't give a damn about your survival as an individual. Give a damn about the wellbeing of others as if they were you. They *are* you, by the way.

↪ Empower Source
Abundance
Normal
Emergency
Danger
Non-existence
Injury
Uncertainty
Opposition
Disloyalty

Chapter Eleven:
Abundance

*In Abundance life is a you and me experience.
Everyone associated with you wins. There are no
losers.*

When you move above Normal on the integrity scale, you are in new territory. This is a higher state of integrity than that into which you were born. You were born into a world of scarcity, where things are believed so solidly to be scarce, that almost no one even thinks about it. We don't think "Things are scarce." We think all of the rest of our thoughts from the ground-of-being called "Things are scarce." So we "know" there isn't enough food in the world, we are sure that if one person becomes wealthy, then others must become poor. We even think energy is in short supply!

So, the state of Abundance is one in which you are over-whelmed with the evidence that there is no scarcity. Your project begins to pay off in such a way that everyone involved is winning out of it, that there are literally no losers anywhere in the universe, as regards your project. You become exhilarated and grateful. Life is an enchantment. You welcome problems and your devotion to life is the solution to those problems.

In Abundance you begin to have great clarity about the factors which produce the results in your project. To move up the integrity scale to Empower Source, you merely do more of the same: be on purpose, promote, stiffen your integrity, play the game ethically.

There is only one element missing to propel you to the top of the integrity chart and that is to empower others to achieve their own ascent up the integrity scale. In order for you to fully win, others around you must also win. If they lose, you lose, and you will slide back down the integrity scale.

Chapter Twelve:
Empower Source

There is room for you at the top. In fact, there is room for everyone at the top.

At Empower Source life is magical. You achieve results more or less by a wave of the hand. People come and go at your command and they serve you in whatever way you desire. People love you, admire you and respect you. This is the ultimate in winning through enlightenment.

I don't mean to imply that life is now a bowl of cherries. It is not. It is simply magical. The fact is that as you grow in your own integrity, you become conscious of the responsibility you have in the world. As your power grows, so does your sense of responsibility. It is inherent in the process. Therefore, when you reach Empower Source, the mess the world is in becomes your personal problem. No longer can you say to yourself "Little me is just too little to do anything about it." Given the power other people feed you when you are in Empower Source, you are not just "little you." You are close to being your Self, the Empowered Self we discussed earlier in this volume. You become not just a concerned citizen, but a concerned citizen who takes effective action.

It is very difficult to imagine what life would be like at Empower Source from below that on the integrity scale. In the low regions of the integrity chart you have to think of people in Empower Source as con artists, because that is the only way you can see that *you* could achieve those kinds of results. In fact, if you are in Disloyalty or Opposition, I doubt if you have read this far. But if you are, you will see someone in Empower Source as evil. That is simply a reflection of yourself you are seeing. Life is always like that—whatever you see in others is that which you have within you. If it is negative, then it is that in you which you are trying to hide.

Life should be for everyone as it is for a person in Empower Source. There is plenty of room at the top, by the way. In fact, the nature of this game, the Transformation Game, is that there is room for *everyone* at the top of the integrity scale.

BOOK III
THE TECHNOLOGY OF CREATIVITY

This short book is for you to study carefully and perhaps re-read several times. Since you have never seen the technology of creativity explained, this information will require your closest attention. In truth, it is simple and later it will seem obvious to you.

The next thing I want to leave you with is the ability to cause ideas. If I merely left you with several ideas that would work if you used them, I would have failed in my purpose. I intend for you to become the source of the ideas you have in life. That is, they will become your ideas, and you will experience yourself as the source of those ideas. Beyond that I want to leave you with the ability to generate new ideas from nothing. This involves lighting up something already within you.

Around every issue in life Mind develops positions. Often the positions are conflictual within the same mind. When you bring onto the scene other minds, there is always conflict. You have remarkable ability to perceive the truth. However, when you do it becomes a position, and as such, is no longer something that you can use as an idea, rather you have to defend it from others or from yourself. Thus the forces in your mind are aligned in such a way that you must waste energy being in conflict. This condition springs from the fundamental concept that there is a "right" position on every issue. There is only one way to free your mind from this condition and that is to drop the fundamental concept that there is a "right" position about everything. Thus a condition is created in your mind in which old conflicts are transformed into mutually supporting and nurturing knowing. In this condition ideas that work are available to you in everlasting supply. One could call this creation of a context to generate ideas.

None of us have a corner on the idea market. Ideas are there and available to you. They merely await you to create the context for them to be. By reading this book you demonstrate your capacity to hold ideas. If you were unwilling to realign the forces in your mind you could not have made it past the introduction.

Geometrically, the realignment of forces within your mind that *prevents* a space for ideas to be, looks like this:

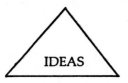

"Important" beliefs

and

"Right" positions

The circle below represents you and the triangle above represents the endless supply of ideas available to you, if you are willing to realign your mind to create a space for them to be in your awareness. But, notice that in this alignment you have no direct access to ideas. All avenues are blocked by "important" beliefs and "right" positions. The manner in which you hold this alignment in place is by thinking your beliefs are important and your positions are the right (and only legitimate) ones. That is, you hold a concept that your beliefs and positions are outside of you as if they were a real part of the universe and not created by you. In this alignment you are small and have no chance of including and becoming the source of ideas that work.

After you have realigned your mind, which you do by dropping the "importance" of your beliefs and the "rightness" of your positions, you experience a shift in context which allows you access to the endless supply of fresh ideas that work. Geometrically, after realignment, it looks like this:

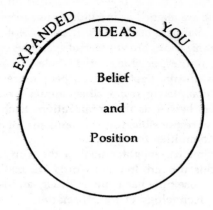

Notice that you will still have your beliefs and positions. They are simply *within* you, rather than outside you, so that there is a clear channel between you and ideas. Ideas are actually now *inside* an expanded you. That is, you are responsible for them. You do not have to look through the smoke screen of your important beliefs and your right positions to see what they are. Thus you become the source of all the ideas in life, even those you first hear from others. For, you see, if you could not create those ideas from nothing in the first place, that is, if your mind were in the first configuration, you would be unable to see them, even if someone else pointed them out to you. The forces in your mind (important belief and right position) would not allow you to create them.

When your mind is realigned there is literally no idea you cannot have. You become the source of ideas and, as you know, ideas run this world. Furthermore, if you are willing to experience others as the source of ideas, you will not get stuck with the illusion of your own importance. In this condition you can cause alignment of Self through generating ideas and the intent to communicate them to others. When you communicate to others from knowing that they are the source of the ideas that you have, this allows them the opportunity to experience themselves as source. This has happened haphazardly throughout human history. The great inventions and the great movements were ideas whose time had come, another way of saying that people were aligned on those ideas.

When people are aligned as individuals not responsible for the whole, nothing happens of significance, except by accident. Government organizations are wonderful examples of people aligned as individuals not responsible for the whole. No one is responsible. The buck is always passed. When people are aligned as individuals, each completely responsible, miracles occur. Each individual considers herself as the organization. Each person holds herself as totally responsible for the outcome of whatever the organization is committed to doing.

This is the time for enlightenment of the world. Transformation of the world is at hand. In other words, the method for causation of an idea whose time has come is, itself, an idea whose time has come. It is a technology of transformation.

BOOK IV
RELATIONSHIPS

A relationship is transformed when you create a context for transformation of the relationship. This requires that you "see" that the relationship is transformed; especially must you see this when there is nothing of which you approve going on in the relationship. A context for transformation is created by consideration alone.

Chapter One:
The Course Of
An Untransformed Relationship

An untransformed relationship accurately reflects the conditions of the world out of which it came.

Ordinarily in life people attempt to form working relationships with special others, "the one," that particular special person we think will complete us and make us satisfied. What we say about it (which is truly demeaning) is that there is not enough of this person to go around and we had best bind him into the relationship by promise or oath so that when he comes up with the idea that he would like to give himself away to someone else, he will not be able to do so without breaking his pledge. This comes out of an "either/or" point of view in which one person either "has" another or someone else "has" him. This point of view does not allow for one person's gain without another person's loss. It is the foundation stone of jealousy and accounts for possessiveness and insecurity in relationships; it is the most fundamental cause that those "special" relationships do not work.

In the beginning of most "special" relationships each person has an experience of the infinite capacity which he or she has to give and which the other person has in equal measure. This experience occurs out of time and place and is not logically provable, for it merely exists as a truth so true that proof is not necessary. Then: enter Mind, that wonderfully logical machine. Mind surveys the situation, notes that the body of the other individual is finite and immediately invalidates the experience of the other person as infinite. Misidentifying the other person as his mind/body machine, it attempts to bind that mind/body machine into an agreement system designed to trap it for later use. At hand is the downfall of the "special" relationship: you cannot really have what you need or what you are not willing to not have. After that the relationship becomes one in which people are bound by their agreement to be in the relationship, the element of choice is no longer present, and we call the relationship "entrapment." Relating to the other person becomes a pain, an obligation, and the flight into fantasy begins. Wishing and wanting for others washes over you in great tides and the more others are unavailable to you, the stronger and deeper are the tidal currents. Resentment builds on regret and your once special relationship consists of pure sacrifice.

It is important to realize that , as always, there are two positions (position and opposition) in this game and as soon as one person takes a position, that creates the opposite position in the mind of the other person with *mechanical reliability*. One position is that of the entrapor and the other position is that of the entrapee. It really does not make any difference which position you occupy at a given time (the positions tend to exchange anyway) for on either side there are the same fundamental conditions: desperation, dissatisfaction, anger, and a sense of impending doom.

Chapter Two:
Transformed Relationship

The secret to creating a transformed relationship lies in being willing to be the Life Force within which the relationship exists, to give up being merely your position within the relationship.

So much for the description of special relationships that do not work, for now I would like to invite you into the enlightened, contextual way of holding your relationships which yields joy and satisfaction. To reach this you have to give up the idea that you are an individual in a relationship and be willing to experience yourself *as the relationship* and your individuality as a mere position within the relationship. This takes you out of the position/opposition bind and the price you pay is that you do not get to be right in your many opinions and judgements. When an issue comes up for resolution you are no longer stuck with defending your position but rather you are free to look and see what the position or viewpoint of the relationship is, that is what works in the relationship rather than what makes you right and the other person wrong. I call this process surrendering into the relationship. When you surrender you simply give up and say something to the effect of "I trust this relationship completely, so let it tell me what to do and I will do it." Surrender means giving up your fear that you will not survive and the general distrust that fear engenders. This brings you close to the experience of being the context of the relationship which is the next experience after experiencng yourself as the relationship. As you surrender into the relationship you realize that *you are the Life Force in which the relationship exists.* When you make this fundamental shift in your experience from individuality through relationship to the Life Force in which individuality and relationship exist, you become the context, not only of your relationship with this person, but also the context of that person's relationship with all others. You achieve this by giving permission and blessing the other person's relationships so that whatever joy is experienced within those relationships is experienced by you as your own joy. Obviously jealousy and possessiveness have no place in a transformed relationship unless you hold it in a way that validates and contributes to the relationship.

Notice that I did not say that there is not a place for jealousy and possessiveness in a transformed relationship. Mind is a simple machine. By the time an experience, such as jealousy, occurs, it is too late for you to do anything about it. Since we live in continuous successive moments of now, if you have jealousy, then jealousy is what you have. Your only choice, which is the only choice you ever have anyway, is the way in which you hold your jealousy. In the simple machine called Mind there are only three possible ways of holding jealousy: (1) it is terrible, (2) "I do not care," and (3) it is wonderful. I suggest to you that you do have a choice and I further suggest to you that the choice that works is that it is wonderful. You can make up your own reasons why it is wonderful and your reasons do not really count anyway, even though they appear to support whatever choice you make. Fundamentally you choose one of the three choices by magical consideration; it is wonderful if you say so and it is not if you say it is not. So you can see that when you choose it to be wonderful when you are jealous and you have a lot of jealousy, you have a lot of wonderfulness in the relationship.

Of course telling you these things activates your fears of loss and non-survival. It reactivates all the Mind garbage that supports jealousy as appropriate. It also reactivates the reasons why people *should* be "true" (entrapped) to one another.

If you and I are in a relationship and I become the context in which your other relationships occur how would I ever lose you? Chances are you would want to stay with me forever, but if you did not, where in this universe would you be able to go that would be far enough away for me not to love you or for you not to love me? I can only experience grief in our relationship to the extent that

I think I own you or have some right to determine the course of your life, that is to the extent that I am attached to the *form* of our relationship. If I am willing to be complete in my relationship with you, which is the same as being complete within myself, I can give you up in the present form of our relationship and love whatever form appears next, even if you move thousands of miles away and live with another person. If you become interested in someone else while you are with me, you can count on me to derive great satisfaction and joy from that; in fact, the satisfaction and joy you ordinarily think of as "yours" is also mine since I am the Life Force in which your life occurs. I am actually entitled to say "I love you," not as a position of attachment and need or to prove how great I am, but simply as a statement of the truth. I love you.

Chapter Three:
Successful/Unsuccessful
Relationships

*Without transformation, without purpose,
every successful relationship is on its way to becoming unsuccessful.*

As an inhabitant of this world, you do not have a choice about whether you will have relationship or not. Even if you live as a hermit in the wilderness, you have a relationship with others which exists within you, the home of all relationships. So, given that you must have relationship, I want to point out the choices.

Relationships fall into two natural divisions: those which are about success and those which are about power. Relationships about success fall into two natural divisions: those which are successful and those which are not successful. Therefore we have (1) successful relationships (2) unsuccessful relationships and (3) powerful or power generating relationships.

SUCCESSFUL RELATIONSHIPS

Relationships which are about success aim to master the physical universe as a final goal, that is, the point of the relationship is survival—preferably survival in style and comfort, but survival nonetheless. In America these relationships are marked by the credit card. Regardless of how well survival is handled, it is never enough because the point of the relationship is to go for success, not to reach success, simply to go for it. Acknowledging that success has been reached would cause a deep sense of purposelessness, therefore the credit card is used to cause the pursuit of the success game to continue. Enormous debts are accumulated. Income never overtakes expenditures.

At the interpersonal level the goal is to follow form. In order to follow form, the relationship evaluates the relationship forms most common in the culture and emulates those forms, taking the common denominators when a choice of forms exists. One lives in a four bedroom house, drives a popular brand car (or an unusual brand), one has children, if that is popular, or no children if that is popular, one is married to one's spouse if that is popular, or simply living together if that is the "in thing." The form changes as time goes by and one generation replaces another, but the pursuit of form never changes.

As regards others—family or organizations, or the world at large—there is little connectedness except as far as those spheres must be successfully manipulated. A successful relationship has a very difficult time dealing with children and family since there is a neat line drawn around the relationship labeled "us first."

Life in a successful relationship is a struggle because the game is never complete—the relationship has never quite survived or succeeded well enough. There is a sense of sacrifice and obligation inherent in the nature of the relationship which the perfect vacation cannot erase for long. And most critically, there is no sense of purpose or contribution to the world, or even to one's own children; there is no sense that the relationship makes a difference, the relationship is turned in on itself, the two people are focused on each other. The real truth is that each person is focused on himself or herself trying desperately to be devoted to his or her partner, or at least appear devoted.

Since there is a neat line drawn around the relationship, there is a natural boundary, or fence, across which to desire others, to seek greener looking pastures. And the other pastures do look greener, other people appear more attractive, more sexy, more nurturing, charming, exciting, than one's partner when viewed across the survival fence. One may not act on one's desires to form fleeting relationships with others, but the desire is always there. There is no hope for the desire to ever disappear.

Within the boundaries of the relationship the game often turns to survival—a you or me kind of experience of one's partner which

goes something like "Since I cannot make a difference in this relationship I will at least make sure you do not either." In other
words, the profound desire all human beings have to contribute to
the lives of others meets its death in a successful relationship and
who one blames is one's partner—not entirely of course, since there
is a rule in successful relationships that each person is 50% responsible. Therefore, it is difficult to escape your "part" in the dif-
ficulties which arise in the relationship. The usual result is a sense
of guilt which is the cardinal signal that a successful relationship is
making the transition into being an unsuccessful relationship.

It could be said that all successful relationships are on the road
to becoming unsuccessful relationships and the only missing ingre-
dient is time. If you will take a look at the basic assumptions of a
successful relationship: (1) our relationship makes no difference to
the world, contributes nothing, (2) the point of our relationship is
to make money and consume goods, and (3) there is a neat ownership line drawn around our relationship which you cannot cross
—if you take a look at these rules and assumptions, you will see
that all successful relationships are on the way to becoming unsuccessful relationships.

UNSUCCESSFUL RELATIONSHIPS

Unsuccessful relationships can be viewed as old successful relationships. They have existed long enough for the natural process inherent in successful relationships to evolve. An unsuccessful relationship has flowered, so to speak, and that which was always
there in the successful relationship comes to the surface, or blooms,
for all to see. The fact of no purpose, no contribution, no difference
made, becomes too obvious to conceal any longer. The fact that
this condition is obvious does not mean that it will be acknowledged—usually it is not. In the usual course of events the relationship enters a dramatic phase marked by covert or obvious acting
out of the hostility which exists. This hostility is a reaction to the
sense of uselessness inherent in the relationship. Arguments become
the usual, rather than the unusual reaction to disagreements. Irrational jealousy flares up; possessiveness, domination, and control
replace mutuality and oneness. Actually, mutuality and oneness
never existed in the first place in the successful relationship, but

even the pretense of mutuality and oneness disappears.

At this point one or both individuals begin to think of leaving the relationship. Since our culture, as do all cultures, binds us into prescribed forms, most relationships which have reached this stage drag on for some time before resolution occurs. Resolution may be delayed a lifetime—some people prefer to exist all their lives in this condition, stuck in the belief that all relationships are like this. There is a popular nationally syndicated cartoon called "The Lockhorns" which appears in our morning San Francisco Chronicle, and the message of "The Lockhorns" is that relationships do not work, that the best you can hope for is having someone to live with and that relationships cannot make a difference.

Increasingly in our culture divorce is selected as a way out of a marriage which is about success/unsuccess. However, people waste years of their lives justifying leaving each other. The second choice, of course is to transform the relationship, about which more later. There is a third choice, and that is to seek counseling, or in some fashion "work" on the relationship. What this accomplishes is to drive the success/unsuccess process backwards, hopefully into a successful relationship again. However we have seen that a successful relationship is merely an unsuccessful relationship waiting for the passage of time to become unsuccessful. With "working" on the relationship you can only hope to manipulate conditions. The fundamental cause of unsuccess is not addressed. That fundamental cause is purposelessness—there is no purpose larger than the relationship itself.

(For a description of the nature of a power generating relationship, review pp. 132-135 of *Winning Through Enlightenment*).

Chapter Four:
Commitment—But To What?

Relationship cannot exist without commitment. However, the quality of a relationship is determined by that to which you are committed.

If you look into your experience of relationships you will find that people are naturally committed. *Everyone is committed.* Variability comes forward only in answer to the question, "Committed to what?" Where relationship is concerned here are the choices to which you can be committed: (1) yourself, (2) the other person, (3) the longevity of the relationship, (4) the relationship itself, or (5) the purpose of the relationship. Parenthetically, you can try to be committed to some combination of these choices, however that sets you up to fail due to the fact that commitment to one very often conflicts directly with commitment to the others.

Now, the interesting truth about relationship is that you *must* be committed and you *already are* committed. However, it is not enough to be committed. You must be committed in a direction which can serve as an organizing principle for your life and for life in general. Anything less will lead you to failure and grief. You can only be fully committed to one of the above choices. Let us look at the result of each of these types of commitment.

COMMITMENT TO YOURSELF

In a relationship in which you are committed to yourself, you ask the question "What makes me feel good?" When you get the answer, you then begin to manipulate the other person to produce that which you think makes you feel good. The other person then becomes an object to manipulate and is no longer a person. Smart people with cooperative partners can play the relationship game by these rules for protracted periods of time. These are classic relationships of survival or success. The cardinal word which describes them is pretense and their major characteristic is disloyalty to others. Romance dies an early death here.

COMMITMENT TO THE OTHER PERSON

Many people have realized the folly of being committed to oneself in a relationship—the transparent illusion that it is—and said something like "In relationships there are only two choices: being committed to myself and being committed to the other person. Since it does not work to be committed to myself, then I should be committed to my partner." Having said this, you are off on another wild goose chase about success and survival which operates in an identical fashion to the first one, only the focus has shifted to the other person. It is the same game played with a different piece. Your life then becomes about taking care of someone who is fully capable of taking care of himself. Here also, the cardinal word to describe the relationship is pretense and the major characteristic is disloyalty. It demeans a person to take care of him as if he were an emotional or physical invalid even if he *is* an invalid by ordinary standards of measurement. It makes him less than he could be, to say nothing of that which you deny the world by wasting your time humoring your play-sick partner. Here again there is little aliveness and you function in your relationship out of being a good boy or girl, not out of your experience of the magnificence of human beings.

COMMITMENT TO THE LONGEVITY OF THE RELATIONSHIP

After you get beyond the tempting but erroneous thought that the purpose of the relationship is one person or the other, it will occur to you than an interesting thing to try for would be duration. the game then becomes "Let's see how long we can make this thing last." The real "winners" of this game make it last a lifetime—"Until death do us part." The grand prize comes at the end when you die or the other person dies and you pat yourself on the back and say

"Well, at least he didn't die alone!" Then, if you really play this game to the hilt, you never consider another relationship and you then wait to die yourself. When you die the whole game is over. Actually, you died when you decided to make the relationship about longevity, only you did not notice.

COMMITMENT TO THE RELATIONSHIP

We live in an increasingly enlightened age wherein many people have been able to see the folly of the first three commitments and have landed on the square called "Commitment to the Relationship." At this position on the game board it appears to you that what you really should be committed to is the quality of the relationship. This is so close to being it, that it is very difficult to see beyond this position. At this stage people seek pleasure together: movies, plays, camping out, champagne and candlelight. The difficulty with all this is that it is all form and substance without an organizing principle. There is nothing to give it meaning—it does not mean anything. So, eventually it turns up empty and unsatisfying.

COMMITMENT TO PURPOSE: THE POWER GENERATING RELATIONSHIP

A purpose in a relationship is an organizing principle which can be stated in a few words, and which, when realized, is a major contribution to human beings. You must see that this is the focal organizing principle to relationship and that nothing else is, that all else is fool's pleasure or fool's pain. You must see that you are not the organizing principle, that the other person is not the organizing principle, that longevity of the relationship is not the organizing principle, that the relationship itself is not the organizing principle. Purpose is the organizing principle which gives life to relationship. Anything else you go for is a sell-out and you will get what you deserve for selling out. That which you sell out is your aliveness and the aliveness of the other person. It is an outrageous price to pay and you would not pay it if you knew it to be unnecessary; people only pay the price of purposelessness out of the belief that there is no other way. Why is this?

This tragic circumstance exists because of the condition in which we live as human beings. That condition could be simply stated "Individuals do not count, do not make any difference, cannot contribute." We think we can contribute only when we have enormous support and agreement behind us. We look into the evidence to determine our experience of whether we count or not. As individuals, therefore, we are relatively sure that we do not count, do not make a difference, and because we think that, we in fact, do not make a difference. Or, said another way, we make a difference by not making a difference. The world knows of our power only by virtue of the fact that it is not expressed.

Thus holding ourselves as individuals, how could we ever realize that we matter as relationship? Since I do not make a difference, neither do we. Our relationship does not matter, so the best we can do is jerk off with it: become consumers and pleasure seekers.

To turn this condition around as a relationship there must be created and chosen a purpose or context. True purpose or context generates another condition, the condition in which you can only make a difference and you can only contribute. Existing in a relationship of purpose or context could be said to be existing in Heaven. If that is not Heaven, then there is no Heaven. If purposelessness in relationship is not Hell, then there is no Hell.

To be true to a purpose larger than yourself, larger than your partner, larger than the relationship, is to be true to your Self, *the* Self, the Empowered Self.

Chapter Five:
Survival Vs. Transformation

*A world that works for everyone, a you and
me world—the creation of such a world is our common purpose—yours and mine.*

Contrasting the power-generating relationship is the relationship which is secure and safe. Often human beings are so completely dominated by the prevailing condition in the world which says
that no one matters, no one's life make a difference, or can make a
difference, and instead, choose a relationship which is safe and
secure.

The ego fears death. In the face of the fact that in life, only
death is certain, people choose to fear the inevitable. If that is not
stupid, there is no stupid. Nevertheless, people fear death. Out of
the fear of dying, people worry about how close to not surviving
they are now and set up conditions to place themselves as far away
from the end of the imaginary life/death scale as possible. Relationships are therefore chosen and managed in a way to recreate the experience of childhood—of being taken care of, in an emotional
and/or financial way, which makes it possible for time to stand still
—for the spector of not being here, of dying, to disappear.
Tragically, your profound desire to make a difference in life, for it
to matter that you lived, becomes subservient to your fear of not
being alive. You spend your life looking for a place to re-attach
your umbilical cord.

To spell out the uncomfortable truth, that which we sell out
for is contained in the following sequence of nouns: money, cars,

homes, furniture, friends, clothes, warm bodies, food, prestige, ability to dominate others, good looks, and you could add to this very long list. If you will notice, each and every one of the things on this list, you think, contributes to surviving a little better or longer before dying. You will have to look at that to see it because we almost never confront the truth about that which motivates us in life. This *motivates* you. these things *are* your motivations. Whether you like it or you do not like it, your desire for these things literally moves you from place to place in life. They dictate with whom you spend time, how you spend that time, even what you talk about. You are completely dominated by this and to the degree that you think you are not, your condition is hopeless. If you think you are not run by this stuff, your life will not make any difference in your own experience. Your energy will be consumed proving you are "good." You cannot afford to lie about this—your life is run by survival/fear mechanisms, unless of course, it is not. But it is. I don't mean to imply that you can't transcend survival/fear mechanisms. I simply want you to be clear that you have them.

This then, the fear of death, is the origin of a you or me world—a world in which, for me to make it some "you" out there has to not make it: a world in which the myth of scarcity of money and food rules the day and the inevitability of human suffering is taken for granted; a world in which one must win by making someone else lose.

At the level of relationships then, a you or me world is an us or them world. The "us" consists of two or more people banded together against the world. A tight imaginary line is drawn around "us," and "them" must not be allowed inside the circle. No matter who they are, they must not be allowed inside in any real sense of that word.

Accepting these assumptions: scarcity of wealth (in the broad sense of that word) and the inevitability of human suffering, and the formation of exclusive, excluding, closed relationships is the ultimate "sell-out." That which is "sold" is aliveness in the potential of relationships. What you receive in return is a sense of security—you are safe (but not really) in a hostile world and all you have to give up is being alive. You can die into your exclusivity and forget Who You Are because you forget Who Others Are.

Viewing this phenomenon from inside the phenomenon one cannot see any other reality. Wealth *is* scarce, people *must* suffer, someone *has* to lose. Even when you can see the truth of the condition of the world, you cannot see how it could be any other way. If it were obvious there would be no need for this book.

The remainder of this book, therefore, will be to allow you to discover your power to make a difference in a you or me, us or them world and your power to transform and participate in the transformation of this you or me world into a you *and* me, us *and* them world. I do not have your answers, but I have been with you long enough to know that You do. What I have is the ability to allow you to discover your Self, wherein all answers lie.

A world that works for everyone, and you and me world—the creation of such a world is our common purpose—yours and mine. And common purpose is the essence of powerful relationships, for commonality of purpose in relationship is what love is.

BOOK V
MAN/WOMAN

The mysteries of man/woman relationships reveal themselves slowly over the course of a lifetime and are sometimes so difficult to discover one could ask "Why bother?"
No reason.

Chapter One:
The House Of Mirrors

*Whatever you think about the opposite sex,
the truth is almost always the opposite.*

The subject of man/woman is unusually difficult for people to handle. Witness the fact of unprecedented numbers of people choosing to remain single and unprecedented numbers of married people choosing divorce. Each person thinks her or his understanding of man/woman is correct and almost no one has the kind of information which allows mastery of relationships at the man/woman level. And everyone wants to know, which makes it even more remarkable that almost no one knows. And furthermore, those who know are not telling—not because they do not want to tell, but because they cannot tell—there is no accepted language in which to tell this kind of information. This kind of information is not like ordinary information. It is information that can only be perceived as a distant image is perceived in a house of mirrors and it can only be taught in the same way. It will be practically impossible for me to say anything about man/woman without going into the mirror house of your mind so that you will think I am saying something other than what I am actually saying. Two things will be of assistance here: (1) suspend for a time the notion that you know anything about man/woman, and (2) notice that I write exactly what I mean. You do not need to interpret what I write—it is just what it is.

Now, you can only look at man/woman from a position. One position is called man and the other position is called woman. Since you are one or the other you *must* look at man/woman from a position. However, in order to see what is so about a subject you must look at it without attachment, without a position, without a vested interest in what is so, but simply to see what is so. You probably do not care if grass is green or blue and if you see some blue grass you will not have any trouble recognizing it. However, if you see something about man/woman, you cannot see it objectively, because you are one of those (man or woman) and you are invested in the outcome of your observations. When you look into a mirror at your own reflection, you do not see yourself as you are, rather you see a mirror image of how you are. Nevertheless, you accept that mirror image as representative of the way you actually appear. The human face has enough symmetry that your mirror image *is* representative of your actual appearance. When you are a man trying to understand a woman, there isn't enough symmetry for your observations to be useful.

When men look into their experience of women (or vice-versa), they want to see whatever will enable them to predict women. Unfortunately, it is impossible for men to look into the nature of women, however it is easy for men to think they can do that. What men actually see is a reflection of themselves, not a true image of women. Men see in women their own nature—that part of it which is repressed and denied. Therefore, men think women are romantic, bleary-eyed, impractical fools. Women are nothing of the kind. Men are, however. Women on the other hand look into their experience of men for the same reason—to predict them. They too see a reflection of themselves, not the true nature of men. Therefore, women think men are strong, practical, intelligent, unemotional, unromantic. Men are nothing of the kind. Women are, however.

In the beginning of each human life, there was no woman-ness or man-ness, there was only an anatomical difference. The context woman-ness or man-ness is learned. Boys are taught to be strong, practical, intelligent, unemotional and unromantic. When you train yourself to be something *you validate that you are the opposite*, otherwise there is no need for the training. Girls, on the other hand, are taught to be romantic, bleary-eyed, impractical fools, thereby validating them as the opposite.

You could say that women are the way men are supposed to be

and men are the way women are supposed to be. However, women usually "act" the way women are supposed to act and men usually "act" the way men are supposed to act. Perhaps now you can see that men view women as in a mirror and not only women but themselves as well. And women see men as through a mirror. Is it any wonder that things go as they do between men and women?

You will never see the opposite sex in any other way. However, with practice it is possible to read mirror-writing. Read this section and you will be able to read the opposite sex. For right now, whatever you are sure is true about the opposite sex is the opposite of what is actually true of them.

Chapter Two:
The Intelligence Of Women

You will think what I have to say about intelligence and the sexes is crazy. But, what do you know?

Men are supposed to be intelligent and women are supposed to be not-so-intelligent. I am not referring to the I.Q. test variety of intelligence but to real intelligence as it applies to relationships. This kind of intelligence is measured by the ability to look into the true nature of relationship. Women have the ability to do this. Men do not. Women know they have this ability. Men do not. Women have an unspoken agreement with each other not to reveal that they have this kind of intelligence.

The result of having this kind of intelligence is that women are usually in control of men and women are always in control of the events of a man/woman relationship. There is a secret agreement amongst all women to never reveal this information. In fact, this agreement is so sacred that if you take this truth and go ask a woman about it, she will deny it absolutely.

Men think women want them to be smart, not realizing that all women see the true stupidity of all men. Women do not love men because men are smart. Women love men despite their stupidity. Women do not crave after a smart man, rather after a *trainable* man, one who knows that he does not know it all and is willing to listen to the lessons women have to teach. Women want to manage and take care of this not-so-smart creature called man and they look for those characteristics in a man which make him amenable to being taken care of and managed. Do you know that in these "liberated" times, women do 30% of the work (gainful employment) and control 70% of the spendable money? Need I say more?

Now, unfortunately some women have bought the notion that they are not intelligent and therefore these women do not take responsibility for being intelligent, and actually act stupid. Nevertheless, as you observe a woman's "stupid" behavior it reveals her as supremely intelligent, even if it is manifested in acting dumb with great intelligence. This "act" is adopted to protect men from the devastation of finding out how second rate male intelligence is by comparison. It is also used as a way of being in even more complete control of the course of a man/woman relationship.

Of course I know that you think all of this is not true, that I am just making this up. But, given your history with man/woman, what do you know? Next to nothing, I would say. I write this material especially for women, since men are too stupid to see the truth of it. Since I am a man, there is only one credible source for me to be telling you these things: innumerable women have revealed this information to me.

Chapter Three:
Beginning And Ending
A Relationship

*Women begin and end relationships and ar-
range the appearance that macho man did both.*

We all know that men start relationships and that sometimes
women end them and sometimes men end them. Obviously this is
the truth. Except that it is not.

Men are so stupid, they actually think they choose the women
with whom they become involved. All women know that men have
no choice to even notice them without the woman's cooperation
and consent. Women have the inherent ability to turn men on at
will and men can do nothing about it except notice when it is happening. Women also have the inherent ability to turn men off and
again, all the man can do is notice that it is happening. Women are
very clear about what it takes for a woman to attract a man. Men
are incredibly stupid about what it is about a man that attracts a
woman and therefore most men have little predictability in attracting women. So a woman starts a relationship by simply putting out
her magic and attracting the man. It is magic as far as the man is
concerned because to him it seems that he simply looked across a
crowded room and saw her, not realizing that she planned it that
way. Then the man saunters across the room, and says something
like "Howdy ma'm, let me show you how smart I am and how
tough I am." The woman thinks "Not another one of those" and
says "Oooh. Wow! What a man!" or words to that effect. The man
thinks "She is certainly impressed with me" and says "How about a
drink!" And so begins the relationship. Change the circumstances

and vary the exact wording and you will have the beginning of a man/woman relationship in our culture. The beginning is totally orchestrated by the woman and this includes having the man think it was his idea.

Then the course of the relationship occurs, that is the middle. The nature of the middle of a relationship is that the woman is testing the man to see of what he is made. She is testing him to see if he is the White Knight for whom she has been waiting. Most men fail the test and therefore there is an end to the relationship. The woman brings this about also, not always consciously, however. Most women are aware that they start relationships. Few are aware that they end them. It looks like the man ends the cycle and he usually thinks he does. However, although it is on the man to end the relationship formally—usually by leaving—the truth is that the woman has tested the man and found that he does not measure up, is not the White Knight and has discharged him from service. Ordinarily women do this by driving the man away by being mean to him, about which more in the next chapter.

Chapter Four:
Mean

A woman is meanest to the man she loves most.

Most men have noticed that women have a mean streak. However, men are stupid and almost all have assumed that the meanness they have experienced from a woman was unique to *that* woman and *that* relationship. It is not. Women are mean to men. They may cover over their mean with a "nice act," however that is just another way of being mean. Women are angry with men for the personal repression and gross discrimination they have experienced all their lives. Women have been second-class citizens and they are angry about it! If you are a man, the closer you are to a particular woman the more of this anger you will receive. And there is no maybe about it. You are going to get it. As you get closer to a particular woman and your devotion to her becomes more obvious to her, she correctly perceives that it is safe for her to express her anger, and she will express it by being very mean to you. She will gripe, complain, withhold affection, withhold sex, make you wrong in front of your friends, in short damage your ego in an variety of creative ways. She will burst into tears at the very moment you thought she was going to be happiest. She will say she wants sex but not bother to turn you on. You will think you are impotent and inadequate.

I want to emphasize that this has nothing to do with you. It has to do with a lifetime of repression, of being ignored, treated second-class, of seeing little boys treated first-class. Women, gentlemen, are angry and mean, not because they want to be, but because they are. You cannot escape this. When you are close enough, trusted enough, you will get it. I promise you. No matter how good-looking you are, no matter how charming you are, when you are close enough to be trusted not to leave, you are going to get plenty of mean. If you leave that woman thinking that other women will not be mean to you, you are in for a *big* disappointment. They are *all* like that! In fact if your woman is mean to you, congratulate yourself for being trustworthy enough for her to express her lifetime of resentment to you. All true White Knights take a lot of mean in the course of their relationship with The Princess.

In the stage of a relationship in which a woman is mean to you, two things are going on: (1) the woman is expressing herself and (2) you are being tested. It is a privilege to have reached this stage. Be glad you are there. Love her. Stay with her.

A mean woman does not want to be mean. She knows she is wasting your precious life with her meanness, and remember, she is also wasting her own life. And she knows it. She does not want to be mean to you, and she needs to know that you understand at a deep level where her mean is coming from before she can give it up. And she *will* give it up unless you get stuck in a position of blaming her personally for it, in which case it will persist as long as you blame her. Women are not hopeless. Men are sometimes hopeless but women are always ready to get off it and get on with it. Women will give up their mean if you will: (1) stop blaming them for it, be responsible for it (you are one of the people who cause it) and (2) let her know that you know where it comes from and that she is entitled to be mean. By the way, if you were treated as a second-class citizen, you would be mean too. In fact, men who have been treated as second-class citizens (minorities) are, in fact, mean as Hell, just like women except that, being men, they are less dangerous.

As the man, what you have going for you is that you are a gentleman. If it came to a contest to see who could be meanest, you would win. However your job is not to be a bigger bitch than she is, but to be the gentleman you are, so that she can discover the gentle woman she is. Part of being a gentleman is producing for her, and that takes us into the next chapter.

Chapter Five:
Production And Consumption

There are basic agreements in society which you must know about to have a workable man/woman relationship.

Please be clear that I am not referring here to The Truth. Obviously we make up what appears to be reality by the presuppositions or principles we create about it. So, what I am telling you about the nature of the relationship between men and women is not true before you say so, and it *functions* as The Truth after you declare it. Given that, there is a vast area of presuppositions that we, as society, have created, "said," if you will, and that functions as if it were The Truth. Since you exist in that environment, then you had better be aware that these presuppositions exist, because from these presuppositions are derived the rules by which we all play the man/woman game.

Here is a list of the presuppositions you had better know about and which you had better respect if you want to play the man/woman game with any degree of success:

1. Women are weak, men are strong,
2. Men provide (produce) and women receive (consume),
3. Men are supposed to take care of women.

These first three presuppositions are well-known, not "true," mind you, but treated by society as true. There are other presuppositions which women know about and men do not, and still other presuppositions men made up and women do not know about. These are not as universal, nevertheless you need to know about them in order to play the man/woman game successfully. The other chapters in this section are about those presuppositions. This chapter is about the obvious ones listed above.

I know that these three presuppositions are in disrepute now. Nevertheless people treat them as the basic truth while giving lip-service to more "enlightened" points of view having to do with sameness and equality. In my view, sameness and equality as operating principles are a temporary phenomenon. You do not really think men and women want to be the same, do you? And you cannot have true equality unless you do have sameness. Although the differences between men and women are created, they are real once they are created. Men think in a linear "logical" fashion. Women think in a wholistic "intuitive" fashion and that *is* the way it is. That makes men *"strong"* and women *"powerful"* and you had better understand that. Women *are* the source of things happening and men *are* the instruments of change. A woman without a man is power without means to express itself. A man without a woman is an expression without power. I do not mean to imply that men and women need to be in traditional marriage relationships to express themselves through each other. Merely having contact with the opposite sex gives women a means to express themselves and men a guiding light to know what to express.

As usual, we have set it up to appear the opposite from the way it is. Man/woman is a house of mirrors. It appears that men create direction and women provide the work to get there. That is only the appearance. The underlying truth is that women run the world and use men to carry that out. Things are not the way they appear to be. The movement of women into the professions in recent years represents the fact that women are concerned about the way men are running things and they consider men to need closer supervision. When I say "they," I do not mean individual women—I mean the gender "women"—all women, that is, the collective consciousness called "women."

To the degree that you can realize the true nature of man/woman in a particular relationship, you can create a powerful man/woman relationship. Most of us resist this to the hilt. Powerful man/woman relationships are rare. In fact there are two sets of conspiracies set up to prevent this, about which more in the next two chapters.

This is the basic information you need to get: women are powerful, men are expressive, men produce and women consume, and men are supposed to take care of women. You had better believe it! Too bad guys.

Chapter Six:
The Conspiracy Amongst Men

"I've got one and you haven't: Macho Man."

Men look at women as inferior beings. Sometimes, and in some places, this is openly acknowledged and in other times and places it is not acknowledged. Whether acknowledged or not, it is the way it is. If you are a man you either think women are inferior, or you are one step more unconscious than that: you think all of the rest of your thoughts *from* the thought that women are inferior. You may never think "women are inferior, I know they are," you may only think everything else you think about women with that thought as *the* underlying un-thought-out, unexamined assumption. You may have another "enlightened" thought called "women are equal" and if you accept that as your most fundamental thought on the subject you are a doubly-damned liar: you lie to yourself as well as to others.

Men are born with a tag of tissue between their legs which we make much too much significant. In fact, it is a tag of tissue, nothing more. Nevertheless, we have said "This must mean something" and, having said that, we believe it. It might as well be a statement of The Truth, since we have treated it as meaning something, even though it does not.

So little boys grow up being taught they are strong, fast, smart, etc., because they have this tag of tissue between their legs (of which they are also taught to be ashamed and hide). As a result of this boys secretly think "I've got one and she doesn't," which is true, but then he thinks *"Therefore, I am better."* He thinks this because there is plenty of agreement about it and there is plenty of agreement about it because plenty of us think it (although we never say it).

The result in adult life is "Macho Man," a person who feels, and has been taught that he is better, faster, smarter, stronger. Only he knows better, therefore he feels obligated to prove it all the time, especially in relationship to women. I mean to convey that this is the way it is with *all* men at some level. Some of us have managed to hide it somewhat, to have "enlightened" thoughts over it, nevertheless, if you are a man, you are, in some degree, a "Macho Man." If a woman loves you, she loves you *despite* this, not because of it.

"Macho Men" (all men) have a conspiracy and the conspiracy is to keep women down and in "their place." They (women) are allowed to have jobs, but jobs that are poorly compensated. When they attain equal position with men, they are usually underpaid. Those who attain equal position and equal pay are considered "masculine" no matter how "feminine" they are.

"Macho Men" belong to what I call "The Club." The way one gets into this club is by being born with this tag of tissue between his legs. Then one treats other people *without* a similar tag according to a different set of rules than those people *with* a similar tag of tissue. If you are a member of "The Club" you can go anywhere in the world and receive preferential treatment. It is the second largest club in the world, second only to the "Women's Auxiliary." Men have a true conspiracy against women. The conspiracy is to keep them in the role of second-class citizens. We have token women in high positions as a way of concealing the conspiracy, however there is no concealing it.

All men are "Macho Men" and they all belong to "The Club" and they are all part of the conspiracy. Those who appear not to be part of the conspiracy are concealing what men are up to. We have assigned them to deceive women and they do it so well they do not know they are doing it. Obviously, I am speaking of a collective consciousness here: "Men's Consciousness," which is not available to each and every individual man.

Women are not fooled however and have formed the Women's Auxiliary as a countermeasure. On the other hand, men have formed The Club as countermeasure to The Auxiliary. This is a chicken/egg riddle, for The Club and The Auxiliary sprang into being simultaneously when our ancestors began to live together in family units.

Chapter Seven
The Conspiracy Amongst Women

The inferiority-ness of women is a contextual thought and will continue as a contextual thought until equality for women transforms from a good idea into an idea whose time has come. Ponder that.

As a reaction to and a cause of The Club, women have formed The Auxiliary. The purpose of The Auxiliary is to not let The Club get away with its purpose (to keep women second-class citizens) without paying a heavy-duty price. Women, as a gender, have swallowed whole the notion of their inferiority. Few women question this notion and those who do question it do so within the confines of the thought that it is probably true. This is what I call contextual thinking, that is the evidence one can think of validates the context. In this case the context is inferiority-ness of women.

By the time a female child has any notion that she is a person, separate from other persons, she already has notions about how she is. She is: dainty, unexpressive, soft, emotional, and unintelligent. She plays with things which are not used to do a job but are used to serve other people. So, while her little brother is playing with an erector set, she is playing with a doll which requires a diaper change. She does not choose these types of toys, she is presented with them. So, she develops that part of her brain which is adept at dealing with serving people: the intuitive right cerebral hemisphere. Therefore, while she is learning to act as if she were not intelligent, she is becoming extremely intelligent in an intuitive way. However, she is never validated for this kind of intelligence and learns only much later in life that boys do not have this kind of intelligence.

Despite her intelligence she is invalidated from an early age and all the while her male counterparts are being validated, praised, and doted over. She soon learns that she is a second-class citizen. And she resents it. Part of her conditioning, however, is never to express her resentment, so she becomes demure and forms a silent bond with all other females. As she grows older she learns that, in order to really make it in the eyes of other people, she must form a lasting relationship with one of "them." So, the enemy must be engaged. Somehow she must discover how to admire and respect one of those people she resents. The resolution is rarely complete.

As a member of The Auxiliary she is obligated to watch out for the interest of her sister members vis-a-vis "them" (men). One of the cardinal rules of The Auxiliary is that the existence of The Auxiliary is never revealed. Usually women will not even talk about their secret bond to each other, some do not even "know" about it, even though it expresses itself in thought and deed. The Auxiliary represents a potential revolution in human awareness. This revolution will occur much faster than the Black Revolution because, in this case, the average member of The Club has a member of The Auxiliary in his bed every night. In the case of the Black Revolution of the 60s, most of the revolutionists lived in a different part of town from other folks.

The revolution which lies in potential is that of true equality for women. So far, what we have seen has been equality as a good idea, not as an idea whose time has come. When equality between the sexes becomes an idea whose time has come, there will be a radical change in the education of women from the cradle forward and the level of responsibility filled by women will expand incredibly.

In the meantime, The Auxiliary functions to prevent men from getting away with discrimination without paying a severe price (refer back to the chapter on "mean").

The Auxiliary and The Club will dissolve together, since the existence of each one depends on the existence of the other. This will happen when true equality between the sexes becomes an idea whose time has come. That time is not yet. In the meantime, to play the man/woman game successfully, you must learn how it is *now*. How it is now is that there are a couple of conspiracies going on, one of which you are a part.

Chapter Eight:
Sex: Everything You Always Knew,
And Hoped Was Not True

*The male ego of Macho Man is a fragile thing
and all women know it.*

Contrary to popular myth, people know very little about sex. Men do not understand about women and women do not understand about men. Many men do not even know where a woman's clitoris is located and those who do know do not know what to do with it once they find it. Women tend to know a bit more about what to do with men than that (but not a lot more), however because they are also unsatisfied by their men, they rarely exercise what they do know.

Almost every man thinks he is a great lover and almost every man is not. Women, on the other hand, are too busy faking having a good time with sex to teach men what to do and how to do it. Women fake pleasure, and frequently fake orgasm, because men are devastated upon finding out that sex is not satisfying to a woman. Most women would rather keep their men and fake pleasure than take the risk of telling the truth and having their men leave. The male ego of Macho Man is a fragile thing and all women know it.

If you talk to an individual man, he thinks, of course, that *his* woman is the exception, that she really *does* have a lot of pleasure with him, that she really has great orgasms with him. The truth is that women fake orgasm so frequently that few men know what a real orgasm looks like. Here is a hint fellas: if she is breathing like a race horse and moaning loudly, she is probably faking it. She just wants to get it over with so she can have a little peace. She loves you too much to tell you because she is afraid you will leave if she does. I know you think you are the exception. You probably are not. I advise you to get a formal education about sex. However a good sex education is practically impossible to come by, since sex is so severely suppressed in our culture. The next best thing is to persuade your woman to teach you. To do this you must convince her that your fragile male ego can take the news that you have something to learn.

Where you women are concerned, you need to educate your man in a gentle, supportive way. Simply show him what to do and progress from one step to the next by giving a win for what he is already doing: "That feels great, now do it *this* way," and show him what "this way" is. Have him touch you with the pressure that feels good to you and in the places that feel good to you. Do not make him guess what to do. Guys rarely guess right and no one has ever taught them. As you progress, ask him to educate you to what feels good to him. You do not know all there is to know about male sexuality, naturally, since you are a woman.

Fellas, here is a bit of information you need to know. When a woman leaves a man it is for one of two reasons: (1) he is not being adequately productive with his work to satisfy her appetite or (2) he does not satisfy her sexually. If you satisfy her sexually, she can overlook a lot of other faults. If you do not, then the smallest fault assumes huge proportions in her eyes.

Regarding sex, fellas, you need to know that there is only one kind of orgasm and that is a clitoral orgasm. Women do not have true orgasm from sexual intercourse. Women have orgasm from proper treatment of their clitoris. There is no such thing as a vaginal orgasm. If your woman seems to be having orgasms from intercourse alone (without clitoral contact) she is faking it and you had better wake up to that fact.

All in all, it is amazing that men and women make it together considering the ignorance which exists around the subjects of male sexuality and female sexuality. Women and men can educate each other about this, however women must be willing to quit faking and tell the truth and men must be willing to be taught.

This is not an exhaustive report on sex. My purpose is not to fully educate you about sex. I couldn't if I wanted to, however you *can* find a teacher of the opposite sex and it is in the hands of that teacher that you can learn about sex.

I give a workshop entitled Empowering Man/Woman Relationships. If you are interested, write me for a schedule of workshops in different parts of the U.S., Canada, and other countries. Write in care of:

Context Publications
20 Lomita Avenue
San Francisco, CA 94122
(415) 664-4477

BOOK VI
HUNGER IN OUR WORLD

To end hunger in our world requires both thought and action. One without the other is either useless or ineffectual.

The end of hunger is now an idea whose time has come and is therefore inevitable.

Book VI is an invitation for you to educate yourself at many levels about hunger and to participate in ending it.

The principles which enable us to end hunger are the same principles that transform our personal lives.

Chapter One:
The Context For Ending Hunger

If the end of hunger does not reside within the individual, it does not reside anywhere.

If you read this section (Book VI), you will know the truth about the causes of hunger and starvation in our world. You will have the information which will empower you to make a difference in the problem of the persistence of hunger and you will discover that scarcity of food is *not* the root cause. You will find out that population expansion is not the cause, and you will be confronted with the fact that human suffering is not inevitable. You will also see that there are no true villains in the problem of starvation and you will know that 20 million human lives are lost to starvation needlessly every year in the face of the ability of humanity to feed itself.

You will discover all this and more and it will not make any difference unless you take personal responsibility for it and *act* to bring starvation to an end. In a world which allows a person to write a letter that can reach the other side of the globe in a matter of days, in a world wherein the indivdual can pick up a phone and call another country in a matter of minutes, in a world wherein satellite communication is the order of the day, in a world like this, we must stop saying that the crummy individual does not make a difference. We must also stop saying that some individuals can make a difference and others cannot make a difference. We must also see that churches, governments, and corporations, are made up of individuals and that these individuals are separate from each other and that each one, at the base of his or her Self, wants a better world, a world in which no further deaths occur due to starvation.

The realization of a world without hunger resides in the individual—within you right now, at this moment—that starvation is not inevitable, that action on your part makes a difference. When you know these things, as you will when you finish Book VI, you *will* act on behalf of the problem of hunger and the action you take *will* make a difference. If the end of hunger in our world does not reside within the individual, it does not reside anywhere.

Chapter Two:
Making An Idea's Time Come

First, state the idea, then live your life consistent with your statement by communicating to others and by taking action.

Apparently all is hopeless. Apparently anything any of us ever do ultimately gets lost in the morass of everything everyone does and it all averages out to nothing. Apparently we are all molecules in a cup of water, moving randomly and cancelling each other out so that no one of us can make any difference. No one can get outside the cup. In such a condition the wise thing to do is to stop moving, or at least move randomly and without purpose and this is what most of us are doing about most things in our world. Even great leaders who think they make a difference seem to be cancelled out by other great leaders who think they should make a difference in the opposite direction. This is the condition of human life *and it should be*, given that we are dust and we return to dust. Since we end where we begin, everything should cancel out.

All of this is true and it does not dictate to us how we shall play the game while we are alive. At the base of every human heart resides the profound desire for an end to human suffering. There are people reading this book right now who wish it were true that hunger could end and they know that it cannot, I mean they *know* it. So, the question becomes "How does one *cause* the end of hunger?" As it turns out many human problems of the past which were thought to be inevitable, have turned out to be solvable, *but only when the solution became an idea whose time had come*. The end of small pox, for example, occurred 200 years after the means, that is the vaccine, to end it was developed. Small pox existed in the framework of inevitability until around 1950 when the end of small pox became an idea whose time had come. Everyone knew that placing a man on the moon was impossible in our lifetimes, until the idea's time came in the 1960s. Many of you who read this now take space flight for granted, but there was a time when the attitude was "If God had meant for man to be on the moon, he would have put us there." It was as impossible as the end of hunger seems today.

How then does one make an idea's time come? If we could make the end of hunger an idea whose time has come, then the beginning of the end of hunger could be said to exist. So, how does one make an idea's time come? The answer is so disarmingly simple, I am embarrassed to tell you. You make an idea's time come by saying, for example, "The end of hunger and starvation is an idea whose time has come." Then you live your life consistent with the truth you have stated. John Kennedy stated in the early 1960s, "There will be a man on the moon by the end of the decade." People disagreed about whether it could be done, about whether it should be done, about the means to do it, and so on. Even in the face of opposition, in fact empowered by the opposition, there was a man on the moon before the end of the decade.

So, an idea's time comes when you say so and live consistent with your statement. If there is a secret to making things happen in life this is it. All ideas have opposition, therefore there will be opposition to the idea of ending hunger. Some will think it can not be done. Others will think it should not be done. Many will think that if it is to be done, God will do it. How can all these positions contribute to ending hunger?

To answer this question, we must remember that at the base of every human heart is a profound desire for the end of needless human suffering. Regardless of what people believe about whether or not it can be done, should be done, even within those who see it as "right" that some people suffer and starve, there is a profound desire to see an end to human suffering. Even the vengeance in the heart of a criminal is resting upon this desire. Man's inhumanity to man does not spring out of human nature, but rather out of misinformation. Our beliefs in scarcity and inevitability subvert and prevent the expression of our nature.

Therefore, when you realize this, you realize it by examining your own heart, the heart of a human being. If you knew that hunger was not inevitable, that there is no scarcity, that over-population does not account for starvation, that your lot would not be diminished, but greatly increased by creating the end of hunger, and you knew as a certain fact that it could be done, you would act and you would act now, on behalf of human beings. You would also know that other human beings would act, given the facts, and you would be certain of the outcome. Clearly then, what is missing are the facts. Given the facts you can count on people to take effective action. It may not be the action you agree with, the action *you* would take, and it may even be action that looks counter-productive. Nevertheless, action taken in knowledge of the facts this book will present to you, will be effective.

You then, when you know these things, are a vessel which contains the beginning of the end of world hunger. By communicating these facts to others you create further vessels wherein is contained the end of hunger, each vessel complete in the way a hologram is complete. If you take a holographic plate and break it into many pieces, each piece still contains the original image in its entirety.

You are the end of hunger and this book contains the information which will allow you to make a difference, as an individual.

Chapter Three:
The Statistics

The statistics of starvation will haunt you, and they should. But human beings do not die statistically; they die one by one, painfully, needlessly.

The statistics about the loss of human life to starvation and malnutrition are not the only facts of the matter, however they come out of the other facts and are important to keep in mind, to realize the full significance of the problem. Since starvation seems to occur in someone else's country, it is easy to think of it as occuring in another world. However the truth is that we live in one world—artificial, imaginary lines drawn on a map around land masses not withstanding. It is our world, *your* world in which human beings perish from starvation. There is a basic, fundamental human right which people have, to which we are not being true: the right to sustain one's life from day to day and to have enough food to do that.

In your world 15 to 20 million people lose their lives to starvation every year. This is *two hundred times* the number of people the Rose Bowl will hold when filled to capacity. It is the equivalent of *20 large American cities.* It is literally a mountain of people. It is equivalent to having a Hiroshima every three days. All this happens in your world.

Furthermore, three-quarters of these people are children under the age of six years. That amounts to 28 people lost per minute, 21 of them are children. Is it any wonder that we are unconscious of the full magnitude of this tragedy? Is it any wonder that we have devised beliefs in scarcity of food? Is it any wonder that we have made it up that human suffering is inevitable? With statistics like these, we must either rationalize our inaction or act decisively and act now. Most of us have simply become unconscious of the problem. Since it is supposedly inevitable, we might as well forget about it.

If these figures haunt you, they should. Twenty million lives lost every year. Your fellow human beings. Three-fourths children. Two hundred Rose Bowls. Twenty-eight people per minute.

But human beings do not die statistically; they die one by one, painfully, needlessly.

Chapter Four:
The Facts

The individual, expressed as Self, the Self of all humanity, makes the difference in ending hunger.

There has never been any doubt that we live in one world. Even when people believed that the world was flat, the idea of one world was well accepted. Only in recent times has the irrational idea that this is not one world come into being. I say ''irrational'' because almost no one would argue that people are starving on another planet, however we act as if, we think as if, we plan our lives as if human suffering existed on another world separate from our own. Some religious movements base their belief systems on the irrational idea that they exist in another world separate from others, or soon will. Governments plan, make and execute their policies almost as if each country were in a separate world. Even the artificial division of land masses and cultures seems to be a vote in favor of the idea of multiple worlds.

Politicians speak as if America could protect its interest without protecting the interest of all people. Economists devise plans to cause the success of some countries at the expense of others. We all seem to think we live in a separate world from the rest of humanity. Even our most personal and family relationships are structured to reflect distance, separation, and exclusivity from others.

To realize the truth about our world, you cannot ask anyone, for you will only be told new versions of the same old lies. You cannot create the truth about our world by consulting what you have learned, because you have learned a large pack of lies. You cannot realize the truth about our world *until you know that you do not know,* until you know that you think you know and that your thought that you think you know does not mean anything. You cannot create the truth about our world until you are willing to start back at the beginning, before you became so smart. By the way, if you *are* so smart, why do people continue to starve to death on the same planet you live on?

So to create the truth about our planet, start with unquestioned facts, those facts which no one with a brain would even think about contesting. Some of these facts are:

You live in the same world with all other human beings.

Transportation around the world can be effected in a matter of days.

A message can span the globe at the speed of light.

You can communicate with people from all lands, relatively inexpensively.

The food you eat comes from all over the world.

Organizations are made up of individuals.

Governments are made up of individuals.

Countries are made up of individuals.

The present condition of the world was created by individuals.

You are an individual.

Individuals will create the remaining destiny of mankind.

From these incontestible facts, you can see that your individual unique humaness makes *the* difference in the destiny of the world. Sure there are organizations, governments, international food corporations, and sure these concerns are close to the problem, and sure they are dominated by the patterns and beliefs that operate them; but in a world in which communication occurs at the speed of the light, you are very close to the problem.

If I have anything at all unique to say it is that there are no villains in the problem of world hunger. Even the chief executive of the largest international food corporation is not a villain. He is merely stuck in the same beliefs you and I have been stuck in: scarcity of food and inevitability of human suffering. If he had the experience that he could make a real difference in the problem of hunger, he would give up much more than profit, he would give up his life to make that difference. And so would you.

Chapter Five:
An Introduction To The History
Of Hunger

*The colonial movement set in action the
forces which hold hunger in place to this day.*

Several hundred years ago, we, as humanity, created a colonial movement whereby several rich, powerful, inventive nations crossed land and ocean and planted our power on the lands, farms, and shops of other people—other parts of the human family. We did this as a natural outgrowth of an adventurous spirit and of an expanded technology of travel. We set our governments upon the soils of other nations and ruled them. We brought our customs and traditions and our language. Not as villains, but as human beings, we looked upon those cultures as backward and out of our humanity we did what we could to modernize those cultures, to "civilize" those people. We brought our ideas of agriculture to Asia, Africa and Latin America and, being the forceful persuaders that we were, we persuaded those peoples that it was in their best interest to alter agricultural patterns that had developed over centuries, patterns which worked to feed people an adequate diet. In some cases we disrupted the travel of nomads whose participation in the agricultural systems of the lands they roamed was crucial to the economic and agricultural balance of those lands and the people who lived in them. In some areas we drew lines around land regions and created "countries" where none existed before, all for the purpose of controlling people "for their own good" so they would look more like "us." All of this, and more, happened in the same world in which we live, and the effects are still felt in our world.

We have become so convinced that nothing can be done, that we have failed to inform ourselves about the history of hunger in our world. We are ignorant, not stupid, simply uninformed.

Chapter Six:
The Process
Of Creating Starvation

*Hunger on a massive scale was not created by
an event or by events, but rather as a fluid process,
supported by mistaken beliefs.*

Famines have occured throughout recorded history, however people have never been so vulnerable to famines than at this time in our history. Why is this? Should not our mighty technology cause a buffering effect between drought, temporary food shortage and human beings? It would seem so, but it is not the case. Never before in the history of the world have people starved at the rate we now see. Never before has one-quarter of humanity suffered from malnutrition. Never before modern times have up to 20,000,000 people died from hunger or hunger related causes each year. Why is this? What is happening?

One of the ideas we imported into countries that we colonialized was the idea of exporting specialty crops. Land was subverted for the purposes of producing massive quantities of tobacco, coffee, cocoa, tea, bananas, coconuts, and many other specialty crops which came to be the major crops produced by certain countries. Individual countries stopped growing a well rounded diet for their own consumption and began to grow specialty crops for the consumption of the colonizing country.

One of the startling facts about this process is that host countries did not gain in wealth as a result of specialization of their food crops but rather lost wealth along with the ability to feed themselves. How could this have happened? It happened by centralizing farm land into the hands of a few powerful people. Not villains, but people like you and me, who believed that what they were doing was best for both themselves and their country. On some occasions this process was accelerated by use of the military force of the colonial power, but always in the firm belief that it was all in the best interest of the host countries. It was all done with benevolent intent. *If we fail to acknowledge that, we cannot solve the problem.*

So small farmers who once produced their own food and food for their neighbors, first began to grow lucrative specialty crops and were eventually displaced off their lands by large land owners who in turn hired those farm families to become peasant workers in the fields of large land owners raising a large cash crop for export to another country. These former farmers and their descendants, now peasants, are paid wages by large land owners rather than receiving food as a result of their own labor, as before. People were disenfranchised from their land and the wages they receive are often inadequate to buy food (much of it imported) from the local food market. People who were able to feed themselves could no longer do that because they did not have the land upon which to do it. As time has passed, those who knew how to farm grew old and died and now many do not have the skills to produce their own food, as did their fathers and forefathers. Nevertheless, experience has shown that, given the land, learning occurs very rapidly and competent farmers spring up quickly.

In the process of these events over centuries, giant international food corporations have sprung up to move in, buy the land, import the specialty plant, manage the labor and export the cash crop produced. This is now a multi-billion dollar business and individuals within these corporations control incredible amounts of money and therefore have the ability to influence government policies around the world.

The belief system which sprang up to explain the fact that people seemed to be suffering more as this process continued went something like the following: (1) people are basically stupid and left to their own devices cannot feed themselves and therefore we must take care of them, (2) there is a scarcity of food in the world and population growth will inevitably outstrip our ability to feed people, (3) the development of large centralized farms is inevitable, and should be since this form of food production produces more food and should therefore feed more people, (4) at any rate, human suffering is inevitable and no matter what we do, some people will starve.

It is critically important to see that this happened *as a process* and not as an event. In other words, there was never a time when someone said: "Let's devise a plan to feed a few people and starve others." That never happened. What happened occured as a process supported each step of the way by a belief system which supported the process. The people involved actually believed they were doing the right thing. It may seem stupid to us now, but it is no more stupid than the thought that nothing can be done in the present to end starvation.

I have saved the last belief because it is so firmly entrenched in our minds that it deserves special consideration. It is the belief that "overpopulation" somehow causes death by starvation. This deserves an entire chapter.

Chapter Seven:
The Relationship Between
Poverty And Population Growth

*When you know the facts, you will see that a
high birth rate is a sign of intelligence in a population of starving people.*

There exists a relationship between population growth, hunger
and poverty which is not well understood. People tend to believe
whatever supports a feeling of comfort and security and with
regard to the issue of hunger in our world there has arisen a belief
system which is unconscious and unexamined. This belief system
goes something like the following. "People in underdeveloped nations are naturally inferior. It is too bad that they exist in poverty,
but it is inevitable. If we redistributed all the wealth today, the
money would end up back in our hands in a matter of weeks
anyway due to our superior intelligence. Furthermore, even if
poverty were somehow abolished, hunger would still exist because
everyone knows there is a permanent shortage of food. Anyone can
see that people in underdeveloped countries are multiplying twice
as fast as the rest of the world because they are stupid and do not

know what is best for them. If they would only stop reproducing so fast there would be enough wealth to go around without changing any of the existing economic patterns which cause poverty.''

This theory has it that population growth causes poverty and hunger in the following relationship:

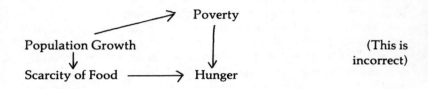

(This is incorrect)

Since we believe that people reproduce at a rapid rate due to incurable ignorance, we also believe that the only possible solution is enforced birth control.

I cannot tell you how absurd all this is. It is all absolutely contrary to the facts. Fundamentally it is a postmortem belief system designed to explain to the simple-minded the puzzling results of colonialization of what are now called ''underdeveloped countries.''

Here is the true relationship between population growth, poverty and hunger:

Poverty ⟶ Hunger ⟶ Population Growth

How can this be? As it turns out, people in underdeveloped nations are not stupid, as we seem to think they are. As the effects of colonialization took hold and the wealth began to flow out of the host countries, widespread poverty set in. Former farmers became laborers and received wages inadequate to feed their families. Hunger became a reality for one-quarter of all people in the world. Parents began to see their children die of hunger and hunger related causes. Since these children, particularly the males, are the major source of security in old age (there is no Social Security in most of the world), and since up to 80% die of malnutrition before age 6, parents are required to have 8 to 10 children to produce one or two living male heirs. Therefore, *as a function of their intelligence,* people in poverty tend to have many times more children than those not so afflicted. The extra hands are needed to work, when there is work, and the sons will be needed in old age. Fortunately for the U.S. we were not a host country after the Revolutionary War and our economy was not exploited for the benefit of other countries. We were able to develop and reap the rewards of our own labor and of our expanding population (work force). Other people have not been so fortunate.

The process for countries such as U.S., Japan and the countries of Europe, those countries which were fortunate enough to be in the forefront of the Industrial Revolution went something like the following. Ever increasing health technology reduced the death rate and therefore increased population. The displacement of peoples from their previous jobs by mechanization created a degree of poverty and uncertainty about life which in turn accelerated the population growth. This process would have resulted in the suffering we now see in underdeveloped countries except that two factors intervened. First, industrialization produced a certain number of jobs which displaced crafts people could perform and receive a minimum wage. Second, the advent of colonialism resulted in the influx of great wealth from the host countries into the colonial powers. Therefore poverty was averted in industrial countries, somewhat at the expense of the rest of the world, and population growth has come under control as a function of the security you and I feel about the probability of a relatively high standard of living and of having our basic needs taken care of in old age whether we have children or not.

The galling truth about all this is that it was never necessary. We did not need to become colonial powers to obtain resources. Resources are in abundance and have only begun to be tapped by our industrial and agricultural processes and they are in abundance in all parts of the earth. This ravaging of other countries itself has come out of the belief in scarcity. Somehow we came to believe that we had to take resources from someone else in order to have an abundance of resources. the absurdity of it all is mind boggling.

A complete diagram of cause-effect regarding birth rate looks like this:

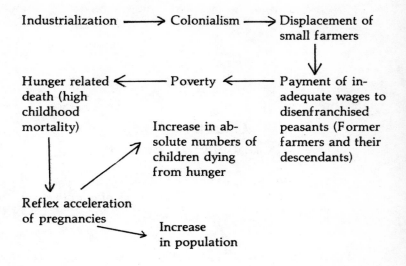

The only birth control that works is alleviation of poverty. Without this, condoms, diaphragms, pills, and education are useless.

It is crucially important to realize that the process causing poverty continues to the present day. Although colonialism no longer formally exists, the agricultural and economic patterns established by colonialization exist in a matrix which is resistant to change, particularly given the strongly held beliefs in scarcity of food and the inevitability of human suffering. I am not going to suggest solutions. You are smart enough to figure those out for yourself. Obviously it means a new economic order. It means a world that works for everyone with no one left out. Only you can create such a world. If you ever find your life boring consider this: there is plenty of work to do which only you can do.

Chapter Eight:
The Belief In Scarcity

It isn't that we think things are scarce. Anyone can see that it is not true. We think all of our other thoughts from scarcity.

When you and I confront the fact that more than 1,000,000,000 people are malnourished in the same world we live in and when we examine our hearts to discover the kind of world we want to live in, the condition of humanity becomes an enigma. Given that our power as a species is so incontestibly great, our mastery over the environment so complete, our ability to create social institutions so well-developed, it is truly absurd that people starve in our world.

There has never been a time when people plotted and planned to create conditions to starve others—plotted to make a profit yes, planned to gain political power definitely, but never has there been an intention for others to starve. How then has it happened? It has happened out of ignorance; we have simply been unaware of the effects of our actions. Nevertheless, there are effects of the actions we take. In the instance of disenfranchisement of farmers through centralization of food producing capacity in the hands of a few, accompanied by the advent of specialty crops for cash export trade, the result has been starvation through poverty. However this was not the planned result—it is merely the unplanned side effect of profit and power seeking. When it occurred, people looked for an explanation. What better explanation than scarcity?

If there is not enough, obviously some people will starve. Then to make it their fault they were starving we came up with the explanation of ''overpopulation.'' If the little so-and-so would not breed so fast, there might be enough to go around so that no one starved. So went the lies. But, not intentional lies, merely reasonable explanations—lies, nonetheless. And you and I believed them and did essentially nothing, certainly nothing effective.

Now, it just so happens that if you believe in scarcity as an explanation for the condition of the world, you are unable to leave it as an explanation for the world only. If you believe in scarcity, you must believe in scarcity for yourself as well. Is it any wonder that in the midst of great wealth most Americans are extremely concerned that they are not making enough money and that no matter how much money is made, it is not enough. You see, you and I have damaged our own lives by allowing the lies to stand. We experienced ourselves as poor! This is a direct result of our world view. So, you can see that there is a certain effect on your life of the fact that people are hungry in your world.

It is not so much that we think things are scarce and it is not even that we think that we do not have enough. Anyone can see that there is an abundance of materials in the universe and most people can see that they have plenty to sustain them. The fact is that we think *from* scarcity. That is, the thought of scarcity is so much a part of the machine we think with that there is never any question of whether scarcity exists or not. We merely think all of our other thoughts in life from the unconscious assumption of scarcity. I know that to have you consider the issue of scarcity and whether or not things are scarce, I will have to rub your face in it through this entire book. I know that you think *from* scarcity and that thoughts that do not come from scarcity seem absurd to you.

There is no scarcity! Agriculturalists assure us that we are producing enough food right now to feed all people and that we have the capacity with present technology (not to mention future technology) to produce twice as much as we now produce. In case you are asleep, wake up and reread this paragraph. One of the things that happens when people are faced with reality instead of fantasy is that they go to sleep. So wake up!

Chapter Nine:
The Belief In Stupidity
And Laziness

*People do not starve because they are stupid
or lazy. How absurd can you be?*

A perpetration is a belief or saying you hold in your mind
about other people which denies others a sense of aliveness. In the
case of poverty the perpetrations we have not only deny a sense of
aliveness but deny life itself. We say that people who are poor are
stupid, that they are lazy. We say that if they wanted to make it,
they would get up and go find a job. We say that entire cultures of
people are stupid and lazy. If you take a guided tour through the
countryside of Mexico, you will see people existing in extreme
poverty and what you will hear the tour guide say is that if they
wanted to eat, they could eat, that they are just lazy and do not
want to eat! And he says this thinking that he is telling the truth.

In the animal kingdom there is not a single creature which does
not know what to do when it is hungry. Some creatures have no
measurable intelligence and yet know that the thing to do when
they are hungry is to eat. And yet, we have the gall to say that
others are too stupid and lazy to want to earn enough money to
eat.

On the other hand, it is understandable that we have these
perpetrations about people who spend their lives in poverty. When
we exist in a world which disempowers us to make a difference
about the problem of hunger, it is at least comforting to think that
those who are suffering somehow choose to suffer.

But I want you to know that it is not so. These things we
believe about people in poverty merely make us feel less nauseated

with our world and have nothing to do with the way things are. There is not a mother on this planet who, when her baby cries in hunger, does not instinctively know what to do. There is not a father anywhere who would turn down a job and see his family starve. People are not lazy, they are weak. You try eating nothing for a few days and see how much strength you have. People are not stupid, although they may be slow because their brains do not receive enough nutriments to think quickly.

And most of all, those in poverty have no voice. They have no way to tell you about their reality and most of us do not want to hear it anyway. I am not kidding myself. This will not be a popular book. People will not want to finish it. It is not pretty. But, for those with the courage to read on, a transformation will occur.

You and I pay a very high price for the fact that people starve. Your personal life is constricted. Out of the beliefs we have which support hunger our personal lives are much less than they could be. You can ignore the problem of hunger only at great expense to your personal life, because you have to maintain the lies about people being lazy and stupid in order to ignore the problem. When you once admit that there is no scarcity, that human suffering is not inevitable, that people in poverty are not lazy and not stupid, you will have to act and you will have to act decisively. If you do not act, you will still be carrying the lies which support hunger in our world.

A "human right" is a privilege that you and I will defend for other people, *all* other people. In the U.S. these include life, liberty, pursuit of happiness, freedom of expression, and so forth. There is another human right which all people have, and that is the right to have enough food, or opportunity to obtain food, to sustain life for oneself and for one's family. This is a human right which all human beings have and it is imminently obtainable. The kind of poverty which imprisons a quarter of humanity cannot be allowed in my world. Having some people eat well and others lose their lives and the lives of their children to hunger is not good enough. I know from first hand experience, and I think you know in your heart, that people do not starve because they are stupid or lazy. How absurd can you be?

Chapter Ten:
Multinational Food Corporations

There are no true "villains" in the problem of hunger.

It is fitting that this chapter be about multinational food corporations, since the economic structure in which they exist has as its foundation the belief in scarcity and produces a superstructure of poverty and starvation. The term "multinational corporation" refers to a large number of business concerns which have business and legal structures in more than one nation. The ones we are concerned with are those which have to do with the production and distribution of food. My purpose is not to name them and to make them out to be villains. They are not villains, nor are they run by villains, but people who, like you and me, exist within a framework of beliefs which define reality. That framework is that things are scarce, people cannot provide for themselves, that people are stupid and lazy and require direction, that human suffering is inevitable, and that starvation is inevitable due to the "fact" of "over-population."

Within this framework of strongly held beliefs, the economic structures established by multinational food corporations are quite reasonable and, in fact, within this framework, the salvation of hungry people lies with the success of multinationals.

It just so happens that large multinational food corporations have more economic clout than the nations with which they deal. This is due to the fact that most countries have specialized in the production of just a few food crops for export and are in competition with other less developed countries to sell those crops. If a less developed country decides it wants a fair price for its export, the multinational corporation can simply go to another, competitive, less developed country and buy the specialty crop from that source. The very threat of this action prevents effective bargaining on the part of the less developed country.

The cash received for specialty export crops goes toward handling the "balance of payments" of the less developed country. This is a large sum of money owed to one or more of the more developed countries as a result of loans of money or technology over past years. Paying on the loan determines future loans which are badly needed. As you can see, the less developed country is not unlike a heroine addict.

Multinational food corporations are not responsible to the people of the countries in which they operate. Instead they are responsible to the shareholders back in the developed countries who demand a healthy, even obscene, profit from the multinationals.

In essence what we have here is a form of indentured servanthood. The owners of the servants are the community of developed nations and the servants are the less developed nations. The system is designed so that the indentured servants never quite make it out of debt, but instead go further into debt. About three-quarters of humanity lives at the expense of the other one-quarter through a system which produces food which is relatively inexpensive due to the fact that the peasants who produce the food have been disenfranchised from their land and written off as stupid and lazy. Our direct instrument for accomplishing this slick feat is called the multinational food corporation.

It is critically important to see that we are responsible for this, not "they." "They" are merely our instruments. Until we see that multinational food corporations are our creations—yours and mine—there is no hope for meaningful change. Whether or not you personally participated in creating multinationals, you are responsible for them. Only you can make a difference about creating a system of equity in which human beings are not written off to die an insulting death or suffer the outrageous pain of the diseases of malnutrition.

It is unnecessary and undesireable for us to go to war against multinational food corporations. They will change from within in due time. Remember that they are made up of individuals, each with a heart, not unlike your own.

Chapter Eleven:
The Medical Results Of Hunger

One should know the medical origin of the appearance of stupidity and laziness.

The length of life a person can expect from birth, as an average figure, is a function of two factors: (1) adequacy of nutrition and (2) adequacy of medical care. Of these two factors, statistically speaking, adequacy of nutrition is by far the more important factor. Adequacy of nutrition can be measured in three ways: (1) number of calories consumed per day, (2) amount of protein consumed per day, and (3) amount of vitamins consumed per day. Usually when the number of calories and the amount of protein are adequate, the vitamin intake is also adequate. Therefore, we will look at calories and protein.

Usually protein and calorie deficiency occur at the same time, but for clarity we will look at the results when one or the other dominates. When the number of calories are not adequate for a normally active life, two things happen: (1) productivity declines and (2) resistance to disease declines. The person loses weight and becomes mentally slow. As a result of the decline in productivity due to inadequate energy supply, poverty increases and the ability to feed one's self and one's family declines even further. A vicious cycle results:

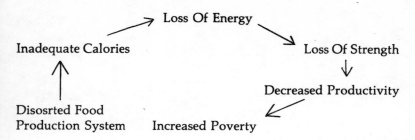

In the extreme, prolonged calorie deficiency produces a condition called morasmus. These people present a wide-eyed, fully conscious stare and appear as living skeletons. Muscle tissue all but disappears and the sharp outlines of the bones are revealed.

By contrast, when protein deficiency predominates, there is a loss of mental ability and awareness as well as a loss of muscle tissue. However the bones are not revealed because water retention by the tissues sets in. The extreme of this condition is called Kwashiorkor. These people appear overweight (due to edema) and present with a blank stare, seemingly unaware of their plight. Again, a vicious cycle ensues.

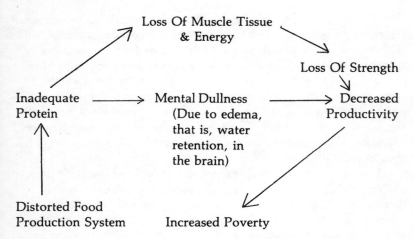

This is not intended to be a medical dissertation. The point here is that people who appear to not want to work, who appear to be lazy, who appear to not be very bright, and who are suffering from malnutrition, are not fundamentally lazy or stupid. People know what to do when they are hungry. They know that they must work to buy or produce food and they know they must eat food to live and produce. *And they want to!* If you think people who are hungry are stupid and lazy, try starving yourself. You will find that even smart, energetic you, will appear stupid and lazy when starving.

I am telling you these things to shake you loose from the idea that people who are poor are poor because they are stupid and lazy. We must wake up to reality: people do not choose to starve and people do not choose to be malnourished or to have their children malnourished. These things happen out of the conditions that exist in the world, the world you and I are responsible for, the one we created and the one we have not changed lately. If you knew you could make a difference in the problem of hunger, a condition that takes millions of human lives every year, you would do anything. If you knew it would make a difference you would give up your material possessions, even lay down your life to make that difference. Fortunately, neither of these is necessary.

Chapter Twelve:
Soft Drinks
In A Hungry World

We cleverly market soft drinks to hungry peo-
ple. Nutrionally, soft drinks are worth nothing or
next to nothing.

The case of the marketing of soft drinks in the less developed countries is not a unique departure from the mentality which governs the marketing of food products in general in those countries. However, it does illustrate a point well enough to deserve a separate discussion.

First of all, it is important to realize what a soft drink is. Basically it is carbonated, artificially flavored, artificially colored water with sugar or a sugar substitute added. Many soft drinks also contain caffeine for a quick lift to induce a state of mild euphoria. The only nutriment contained in a soft drink is processed sugar —pure sucrose. This represents calories and nothing more. There are no vitamins, no protein, no minerals, essentially nothing. In the case of diet soft drinks, there is absolutely nothing of value to the body. They do contain preservatives—of negative value to the body.

Second, it is important to realize what is needed by people whose diet is inadequate. What is needed is protein, vitamins, minerals, all in adequate quantity for maintenance of a normal, active life. None of these is found in soft drinks. Soft drinks actually represent a form of recreation of the taste buds in which hungry people cannot afford to indulge.

Against this background, soft drinks companies have promoted soft drinks in less developed countries, particularly aimed at the poorest sector of the populations. This is done by clever commercials, particularly on the radio waves, since most of the populations are illiterate. American soft drinks are portrayed as the elixir of life, something that healthy Americans drink, something that will produce, and be representative of, a higher quality of life.

As a consequence of this mindless promotion people spend the little money they have on soft drinks, and this subtracts further from the quality of real nutrition they can have. And they think, based on the promotional gimmicks, that they will be healthier if they drink soft drinks. They even feed it to their babies in preference to real food. There is, in fact, a condition named after a certain soft drink which is severe malnutrition in a child fed that soft drink instead of real food.

Actually, the technique for pursuading people to drink soft drinks has been thoroughly researched in the U.S., the only difference being that most Americans can compensate for the intake of this junk with an otherwise nutritious diet. This is not the case for many inhabitants of our planet.

This may sound like an indictment of soft drink companies. It could be made into one and many experts in nutrition do indict soft drink companies for the damage done to illiterate hungry people. I do not indict soft drink companies. In fact, I indict no one. It may be hard to believe, but there are no villains. Soft drinks are pushed on hungry people as a result of the conditions and beliefs we have created, the ones you and I are responsible for, the ones out of which we ourselves live our lives.

The fundamental notion of the condition is that human suffering is inevitable, that if people did not suffer the ill effects of soft drinks, then they would suffer from some other cause. The auxiliary notion is that of scarcity. We say that money is scarce and that we had better get it by any legal means. Most of us are afraid of going to the poor house and starving. Therefore, is it any wonder that we find a degree of exploitation in American business concerns? Is it any wonder that a profit will be taken by any legal means? Is it any wonder that the welfare of hungry people takes a distant second place to the profit motive? In a you *or* me world, which is what most of us create, one person or company can profit only in relationship to the loss of some other person or company.

So, if human suffering is inevitable and we live in a you or me world, then one is justified in doing anything to make a profit. The rules are: make as much money as you can without doing something which can land you in legal trouble. So, many brands of soft drinks are consumed in great quantity throughout the world. The average person in Mexico, for example, consumes five soft drinks every seven days!

Of course it is not true that human suffering is inevitable and it is not true that one can only profit at the expense of someone else's loss. It *is* true that life works much better when one realizes this and it is also true that one's present actions are no longer justified, and it is true that we need to justify the evil we do rather than simply be responsible for it.

The case of soft drinks will make an interesting barometer over the next two decades as a reflection of the transformation of the condition (belief systems) in which we exist.

Chapter Thirteen:
Mother's Milk
Versus Baby Formula

Mother's milk is the perfect food for an infant. Nevertheless we advertise baby formula to be superior, and hungry people believe our lies.

Nature is no fool. Over eons of evolution the human body has developed the most perfect possible method of feeding the human infant. Milk from mother's breast is the complete, perfectly balanced food for the human infant—so perfect that is impossible to improve upon and, in fact, it cannot be duplicated. Nevertheless, baby formula, a substitute for mother's milk made from cow's milk or soy bean is heavily advertised in hungry nations!

Altough nature is no fool, individuals can be fooled. It is only necessary to imply to an uninformed mother that her milk is not as good as baby formula, that her milk is not in adequate supply, that really well-informed people do not breast feed, and people will begin to believe this tripe.

All this and more is contained in the advertising blitz which is occuring in less developed countries. As with cigarettes and soft drinks, the American public is finally catching onto the truth, and consumption of baby formula is on the decline. Faced with declining sales, food companies are looking abroad to take up the lost sales, just as with tobacco and soft drinks.

The result is that people spend money on baby formula instead of badly needed food for the family and ignore the fact that the healthiest way to bring an infant through the first year of· life is by breast feeding.

The truth about the first year of life is that it is the time when a human being is most likely to die from infection. The truth is also that infants in less developed countries are exposed to infection much more than their American counterparts. Mother's milk contains antibodies to those infectious agents to which the child is most likely to be exposed. And finally, the truth is that baby formula does not contain these antibodies. Thus by feeding baby formula, many more deaths are produced in the first year of life than would otherwise occur.

The beliefs which support this practice, usually at an unconscious level, are that human suffering is inevitable and that the individual does not matter anyway. Once again, it is the condition, or set of beliefs, out of which the action comes which is at the bottom of the well, which is the root cause of the action. The condition is the root cause. Individual action, such as promotion of baby formula in the less developed countries, is not cause, but rather is the effect. Belief always underlies action.

Chapter Fourteen:
Tobacco In A Hungry World

We cleverly market cigarettes to people who cannot afford an adequate diet.

Obviously tobacco has no nutritional value. In fact it is an insult to the chemistry of the body and, if anything, would require better nutrition to maintain the same state of health a person would enjoy without smoking. In addition, there are proven long term health hazards to smoking (cancer, emphysema, heart disease to name the obvious ones). Smokers are the best rationalizers you will ever meet. Each one has it figured out that she is the exception to the statistics on smoking, or that the statistics are wrong. Nevertheless, in the developed world, adequate information is disseminated so that smokers at least have the opportunity to confront the fact of damage to their health. As a result the incidence of smoking is declining in America, even as the population climbs.

In underdeveloped countries people are not so fortunate. For the most part governments have not distributed information on the hazards of smoking, nor required tobacco manufacturers to place warnings on their products. Thoroughly trained through their experience with Americans, tobacco companies use the advertising media to promote the notion that smoking is sophisticated, intelligent, a sign of success and excitement in life, and a sure way to attract the opposite sex. People are even led to believe that smoking is not only a sign of success, but a way to succeed in and of itself.

So, who smokes in less developed nations? Is it the rich? The middle class? The poor? Surely it must be impossible for poor people to afford tobacco. The tobacco companies will tell you they are aiming their products at the middle class. Never mind what tobacco companies say. The fact is that in most areas of the third world, one can buy cigarettes *one at a time.* In fact, it is more profitable for the tobacco industry, per cigarette, to sell them one at a time. This allows poor people to spend what little money thay have on tobacco in order to (they think) appear sophisticated, intelligent and successful. In this way people hope to support their families better. And in this way, people waste their health and their money.

Once again there are no villains here. No matter how tempting it is to discover that tobacco people are behind a great evil, the truth is that their actions are sourced by the condition, the set of beliefs to which you and I have given our support over the years: the inevitability of human suffering, scarcity of things (food, for example), and that the individual makes no difference.

Human suffering is not inevitable, there is no scarcity, *only* the individual makes a difference. The opposites are only things you believe. They are true to you, and appear true in the world, because you believe them. Your belief in them perpetuates the conditions we see in the world.

I say certain things in this book over and over because someone must say them over and over. If you believed the sky to be made of water all your life, someone would need to tell you many times over that the sky is made of air before it would stick for you as a reality. I know it is boring, I know it is monotonous, and I know it is necessary.

Chapter Fifteen:
Food "Power"

The "breadbasket of the world" actually has a strangle-hold on the agricultures of less developed countries.

As Americans we live in a fantasy world about the way in which our government uses food in relationship to other countries. The truth of the matter is very complex and it is very simple. It is complex in its exact details and the understanding of those details. It is simple in its overall strategy. To be precise, what we are talking about is the executive branch of our government. We are not talking about a particular president or any particular individuals in the executive branch. Rather we are addressing a certain mentality which has grown over many years and which holds sway over all individuals who enter the executive branch.

Food is the ability to dominate. It really is that simple. the overall strategy of our government when it comes to food is to protect itself and its interests. Food is used to manipulate other governments to stay in political and military alignment with our own.

Food is not used as a means of feeding hungry people. That occurs only incidentally and often does not occur at all. Through much of the Vietnam War, for examle, South Vietnam received almost 50% of all of our food aid while the five hungriest countries of Africa together received a mere fraction of that figure. The government of Chile has been artificially prolonged with the power of the value of food. In other words, food given to Chile is sold by the Chilean government to the highest bidder and the money goes into the general treasury. From there it goes to buy military strength to perpetuate a cruel repressive regime. The cases of South Vietnam and Chile are not the exception but the rule. And it is no secret! It is readily admitted within our executive branch.

Nevertheless, we continue to persist in our belief in America as "the breadbasket of the world" as if we were responsible for feeding the world. As we have seen in earlier chapters, we are responsible for aiding and abetting giant multinational food corporations to carry on a process which deprives peasants of their lands and their ability to produce their own food. We have seen that specialty crops have taken over the economies of many small countries, displacing the well balanced crops which could be grown there, and that these specialty crops are for export to rich countries and that the profits go to the shareholders of the food corporations who live in faraway, well-to-do countries. How magnanimous of us to grant food to needy countries!

Once our food arrives it drives down the price of what locally produced food there is, and deprives local farmers of a fair profit. And furthermore, this food "aid" is by no means free. It is a loan from the U.S. and increases the balance of payments between the U.S. and the less developed countries. In effect, it places other countries in our debt. The result is that those countries must try harder to produce those items which the U.S. imports, including electronics and, more importantly, superfluous specialty crops like pineapple and coffee. This completes the cycle, or strangle-hold, the "breadbasket of the world" has on less developed countries, for at this point foreign governments must do what is necessary to see that the multinational food corporations produce great quantities of export crops for the U.S. What is required is further disenfranchisement of people from their land and from their ability to feed themselves. The strangle-hold looks like this:

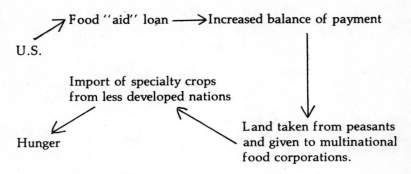

I used to wonder what people were referring to when I read of "American imperialism." I no longer wonder. And, furthermore, I know that I am personally responsible for it and that I caused it by (1) not being informed, and (2) not taking action. I did not bother to inform myself because I "knew" that human suffering was inevitable, that there were no solutions, that food was scarce, etc., etc. In this way you and I have duped ourselves. This is a time for awakening.

Chapter Sixteen
The Green Revolution

In the condition called The Persistence of Hunger, even the Green Revolution caused the persistence of hunger.

Since you have probably heard of "The Green Revolution" I want you to know exactly to what that term refers. In the years 1910-1917 there was a bloody revolutionary war in Mexico fought by peasants and aimed at agrarian reform. In 1910 two percent of the Mexican population owned 97 percent of the land in most states. Over one million peasants died fighting for land. Despite this, little significant reform occured until Lazaro Cardenas was elected president in 1934. By 1940 some 47 percent of the land was owned by small farmers who produced 52 percent of the nation's farm output, and fed themselves as well.

By the end of his administration in 1940, Cardenas had made powerful enemies both in Mexico and in the U.S. Land, producing a source of cheap import food for the U.S., was being given back to the people of Mexico. The large land owners of Mexico managed to gain control of the administration of Cardena's successor, Avila Camacho. The Camacho administration welcomed the Rockefeller Foundation into Mexico and in 1943 the foundation joined with the Camacho administration and began research which became known as "The Green Revolution."

Out of this research genetic mutant seeds and hybrid seeds were developed that produce a higher yield when planted under special circumstances. These special circumstances include massive fertilization and optimal irrigation. To understand what this means for the small farmer, you must realize that, despite overwhelming evidence from all over the world that small farmers produce more per acre than large farmers, political power has been used to support large farm estates. This support takes the form of construction of dams for irrigation of large estates and subsidized prices for large quantities of fertilizer. In essence the small farmer, with his small, carefully farmed plots, is being frozen out of the business of producing food. Dams are not built for small farmers. Governments do not share the cost of fertilizer with small farmers. Thus the development of so-called high yield seeds turned out to be entirely for the benefit of the low efficiency, high technology, politically powerful large farmer with so many acres he cannot manage it all.

In addition, the new seeds, although higher yielding under perfect conditions, are much more prone to disease than seeds which have developed naturally in a particular region over centuries in response to the regional environment. Large farmers can afford the failure of part of their crop due to plant disease. For the small farmer, this represents a catastrophe. Also, hybrid seeds for corn and sorghum do not maintain their genetic purity and must be purchased directly from the manufacturer, rather than produced as a fruit of the harvest. This represents an enormous expense for the small farmer, further excluding him from the food producing system.

This then, is the result of the famous ''Green Revolution'' developed by the Rockefeller Foundation in Mexico for export to all small countries under the influence of the U.S. It has been a boon for the large farmer producing export crops and a reflection of the condition we have created which serves to exclude a section of the human family and condemns them to hunger and deprivation.

It must be becoming clear to you now that the condition in which all efforts to end hunger have occurred could be called "The Persistence of Hunger and Starvation." Is it not obvious that even the most well-intentioned efforts, such as ''The Green Revolution,'' have contributed to the persistence of hunger? In the condition called The Persistence of Hunger and Starvation, everything we do results in the persistence of hunger. It does not matter what we do, hunger persists. Nothing we do makes any difference. The persistence of hunger has been nothing more than a condition in which things happen, or said another way, a set of ideas or, if you like, a set of beliefs.

If we create the context called ''The End of Hunger and Starvation,'' then what we do works to bring about the end of hunger. Whatever course of action you choose to take, as an individual, will work to end hunger if you set it in this context. Even the results of The Green Revolution would work toward the end of hunger. Only the individual has the power to create this context. One creates this context by communicating it. One way to communicate it is to have all your friends read this book. If you read it alone, and do not communicate it, you may as well not read it. Only your communication makes a difference in the creation of a new context.

Chapter Seventeen:
The End Of Hunger:
An Idea Whose Time Has Come

*It requires a transformed individual to create
a contextual idea—an idea whose time has come.*

Transformation could be said to be the act of being yourself, of being free of your opinions—knowing that they do not mean anything—of being free to create your environment consistent with your ideals. To be transformed is to be able to succeed consistent with your own integrity and consistent with what works for other people. It means the certain experience of others as essentially related to oneself, and in truth, the same as oneself.

Of course you have opinions—that is not the point. The point is to realize that they do not mean anything about Reality, and paradoxically, that they create your perception of your reality. When it appears that hunger is inevitable, it requires a personal transformation to see hunger as a reality created by a belief. When you think that there is scarcity, you must be true to yourself and transcend your mind to discover that it appears that way only because you believe it.

I do public presentations frequently about the issue of hunger and I know how people think about hunger. Most people feel that they are too busy to be bothered with hunger and this comes out of being certain that it is inevitable. Others feel guilty about hunger, indicating that at some level they know that their action and their inaction creates the condition of hunger. Others are righteous about the fact that they have plenty to eat and others do not, and these people are defending themselves from the experience of power and responsibility. Others are open to a new idea—"The end

of hunger? What a great idea!" Some do not "believe" it is possible
which is no different than believing anything—it is a "not belief,"
another type of belief. Ironically, it would be just as stupid to
"believe" the end of hunger is possible. One does not believe, but
rather creates the end of hunger. One takes action and creates that
action as effective. If you think you are transformed and you are
not taking action, you only believe yourself to be transformed, you
have not created yourself as transformed. When you "believe"
something, it has an opposite, the "not belief" which you also
believe, except that you deny it. In fact, that is why you believe it in
the first place. When you create a context, it has no opposites. The
contextual idea: the end of hunger is an idea whose time has come,
has no opposite, because there can be only one context regarding
hunger. When the condition was: The Persistence of Hunger, then
hunger persisted and consumed all efforts to end it. Now that the
contextual idea is: The End of Hunger is an Idea Whose Time Has
Come, all efforts to persist hunger serve to end it.

So where can one find a context? Ironically it is where you
least expect to find it: within the individual. LISTEN! WAKE UP!
Things do not just happen in life. Things happen out of the context
you create for them. They do not happen because of what you want
or believe! Only the individual—YOU—have the ability to create
the contextual idea: The End of Hunger. I am amused by the belief
that corporations, or government, or "they" will have to act to end
hunger or it will never end. People actually tend to think that
governments are more powerful than ideas! Can you imagine a corporation more powerful than an idea whose time has come? How
absurd! You have the ability within yourself right now to begin the
end of hunger and have governments and corporations be your servants in that task. Why? Because you are the only source of a contextual idea.

Once created, a contextual idea has the ability to enroll others
to take action. Running, for example, was once *not* an idea whose
time had come. Now running can enroll you. You *support* the idea
of running. If you put on your jog shoes and run down the street,
people support you, they think it is great, they admire you. Why?
Because running is an idea whose time has come. In the process,
running as an idea whose time had come ground up the opposition

and, in fact, the opinions of people who opposed running actually spurred other people into running.

It requires a transformed individual to create a contextual idea like the end of hunger, a person free from domination by his opinions and beliefs. The way we know who is transformed about an idea is that we take a look and see who is taking action. If you want hunger to end, take action.

Chapter Eighteen:
Premeditated Murder

*The worst crimes are those for which there is
no legal remedy.*

Having read this far, you are better informed about hunger
and the beliefs which hold hunger in place than 99% of all people.
In other words, you are one of those people who can act with the
knowledge that you can make a difference. Before you were aware
in this way, hunger persisted—people died by the millions each year
and you were essentially ignorant of the truth about it. I would say
that you were guilty of involuntary manslaughter.

But now you know. If you fail to take action now, I would say
you are guilty of premeditated murder. I do not want you to "feel"
guilty and obviously I want you to take action. What action? *Any
action appropriate to your unique life circumstances.* It does not
matter what you do. Equipped as you are now, anything you do
will work. And, if you persist in believing those beliefs which persist hunger, after knowing the truth and having the choice to create
the end of hunger, you are a murderer—the kind who knows what
he or she is up to, the kind who thinks about it before doing
it—premeditated murder, not of one or ten people, but of millions
upon millions of people.

The worst crimes are those for which there is no legal remedy:
the destruction of a child's self-esteem, the cold betrayal of a person's love, actionless looking-on while a violent crime is in progress. Yet, as revolting as all these are, they are diminished to practically nothing in the face of starvation in our world. While four

billion of us look on, doing almost nothing, 41,000 of us die each day from hunger and hunger related diseases; 41,000 per *year* would be totally unacceptable; per day it is an atrocity comparable to the Holocaust (destruction of 6 million Jews in WW II) every 4½ months. This can only be termed premeditated murder. No other words are descriptive. Anything else we call it only serves to assuage our conscience.

I write these things in the sure knowledge of Who You Are, in the sure knowledge that if you knew your actions would make a difference, you would take immediate, sustained action, that you would not rest in your soul until no more hunger existed. The only thing missing is the sure knowledge that your action *does* make a difference. It does. And you cannot find that out by looking for the evidence. You can only find that out by looking within your Self, the Empowered Self.

If you were convicted of premeditated murder and you paid your so-called ''debt to society'' I would want you to go and live a productive life, to make your life a contribution to life itself, and that by so doing the crime you committed would itself become a contribution to your life and to life itself. Likewise, if you have been taking no action, or action far below your capabilities, regarding hunger, I would want you to now activate yourself, to go forth and take effective action commensurate with your ability. I would want you to play the game of ending hunger as if your life depended on it, for in truth it does. As long as hunger persists anywhere in the world, we will not know what true aliveness can be; we will all be, in a very real sense, dead. If you go into society, into the streets of America, you can see the deadness in people's faces. You and I cannot live unaffected by the deadness we produce by taking no action toward ending this incredible human tragedy. We cannot afford to be premeditating murderers.

Can you imagine the joy and celebration that will burst forth on the day that hunger ends? On that day transformation will be real for you, and until that day your personal transformation will not be complete. On that day, #1 will be transformed forever.

BOOK VII
TRANSFORMATION
IN BUSINESS

The application of the technology of transformation in business so reorders the appearance of business that we are forced to throw out the old models of how business operates. Fundamentally, transformation in business is the shift from competition and opposition to cooperation and empowerment. If there is any notion you have about the way business must operate, then you will have difficulty seeing the shift which is taking place in the way business operates. Here is an entirely new paradigm of business.

Chapter One
The Condition

Until you can appreciate the condition in which you live, the condition of which you are the author, you must stay stuck in the condition as if it were Reality.

In this section I am going to describe to you an ideal business and an ideal way of life which could be termed "Transformation in Business." I am forever amused by many of my friends who talk on forever about transformation in business and continue to participate in a business sytem which is clearly untransformed. By untransformed, I simply mean that the experience of value in life is diminished rather than enhanced by the nature of the business, the rules, the agreements, however you want to say it, in which they participate. We all exist in what could be termed a "condition" regarding the ways in which we make money. A condition is an unconscious unexamined set of beliefs about the way things are and out of these beliefs "reality" is created. An example of one of these beliefs is "no news is good news," or stated another way, "the only real news is bad news." This is the condition in which the news media exists. You need only take in the evening news to discover that the news stories we value most are those that involve death, destruction, and failure.

The condition within which we exist regarding business, work, money, jobs, etc. could be stated thus: "Real success is for lucky rich people who already have it made; they did it by cheating; that kind of success is not available to the ordinary person; people come to be wealthy only at the expense of others who must become poor as a result." Given this condition or set of beliefs, and given that people have an inherent set of ethics, is it any wonder that so few people become truly successful?

This condition is the origin of the job ethic in America. The job ethic states that one should hold a job, work for someone else, for 40 to 45 years and then retire on a pension of about 1/2 to 2/3 of that amount of money on which one was broke before retiring. It really is no surprise that 36 of every 100 men choose to die before age 65 (retirement age). What they die of, of course, is stress related illness: high blood pressure, stroke, heart attack, cancer, or emphysema (usually related to smoking—which people do in an effort to cope with stress induced by working for 40-45 years toward someone else's goals, that is in a job).

Do you know that only 5% of the population makes it to financial independence by age 65? Do you know that 5% are so broke at 65 that they can't retire, but must keep on working and 54% retire on a subsistence income? These are ridiculous statistics, and true.

I counsel people on these issues often and I have found that if you take the average adult in the average situation (broke—perhaps broke making a lot of money, but broke nevertheless) and clearly point out to him or her the principles of success, that person will not be able to even hear those principles, not to mention be unable to put those principles into practice. We have so convinced ourselves that real success is for someone else that it has become, in fact, for someone else.

Freedom, to me, is an abundance of time and money, to the degree that time and money are no longer issues in life, and one has the freedom to live life as it was intended to be lived rather than out of the necessity to make enough money to pay next month's bills. I want the freedom to go where I want, when I want, and how I want. I want to be able to support the charitable organizations which are important to me in a way that makes a real difference. I want the income to give my son the kind of environment in which he can fulfill all of his potential. I have discovered a business which fulfills these and many other dreams and the rest of this section will be a careful analysis of that business to demonstrate the components of an ideal business so that you, if you choose, can structure an ideal business for yourself.

But it won't be easy for you to see this material, for you exist in the condition and until you can begin to appreciate that fact, you will be blind to transformation in business.

Chapter Two
The Dream

Like the Fiddler on the roof, I have a dream...
If I were a rich man, yaba daba daba do...

I want to share with you my dreams, something I started in the previous chapter. I am going to do this not so that you will have the exact same dreams I have, but rather that you can be back in touch with your own dreams. We all had dreams earlier in life about how life was going to be for us when we "grew up." Then we ran into the condition and most of us gave up on our dreams and settled for the way things are. To reclaim our lost power and our lost humanity we must come out of the condition and reclaim our dreams. For example...

If I were a rich man I would make it my business to know other rich people and together we would form a club devoted to a world in which people would no longer have to starve to death. We would work to make others successful as the only way to our own success. When Cambodia came along a few years ago we would have put out the word that we did not have to accept that tragedy and we would have taken action to relieve and reverse the situation. If I were a rich man...

If I were a rich man my wife would no longer have to work and she could stay home with my son and I would stay home with my wife and son and we would live our lives together in love and contentment and when we found out about the starvation that is occurring in the East Horn of Africa, we would have the time and energy to do something about it rather than just say to ourselves "Oh isn't it awful?" If I were a rich man...

If I were a rich man my son would grow up and be educated under my watchful eye and he would be educated in a way that would enable him to make a real difference in the world *right now*, not some vague time in the distant future when he "grew up," although he could make a real difference then too, if I were a rich man...

If I were a rich man I would work hard in my own business the point of which would be to assist others to be successful in their own businesses. I would train them detail by detail until they knew how to do that business so well that they could go train others in the way that I trained them. And I would be available whenever I would be needed and my job would be to be there when people needed me. I would love and serve those people and I would work hard and have fun doing it, if I were a rich man...

If I were a rich man I would travel all over the world *with a purpose* to carry out my business of making others successful and in my travels I would take the time to enjoy the beaches and volcanoes of Hawaii, the stark beauty of the Great Northwest, the majesty of the Alps—I would drink deeply of the world if I were a rich man...

If I were a rich man I would have the freedom to establish my own publishing company and write books for people all over the world and I would have the money and the time to enjoy the relationships established through writing with all those people. I would establish a true network of committed people if I were a rich man...

And I have many friends and acquaintances who have similar dreams and the only difference between my dreams and their dreams, beteween my longings and their longings is that *mine have all come true* and theirs are idle fantasies. And the best is yet to come.

And your dreams can all come true if : (1) you dare to have dreams and (2) you go out and do something. What you do to make your dreams come true is important, especially what you do to make money, so listen carefully to the rest of this section.

Chapter Three
Transformation In Business

Duplication or a win/win business relationship is the essence of transformation in business.

In order to proceed any further you must be willing to divest yourself of the condition. You must be willing to realize that you have been brainwashed by a society bent on keeping you at less that your greatest potential. You must, you must, you must. If you think you know "the way it is" about business and you are not willing to discover that you are hypnotized, then better for you to read no further.

Consider this. A profession I once practiced (medicine, specifically psychiatry) is set up so that if the patient gets well fast the doctor looses income and if the patient takes a long time to recover, the doctor gets rich. Now, there is nothing wrong with psychiatry, however I can't say the same thing about the economic structure in which it is set. If I were inventing medicine I would pay the doctor $10,000 if he could cure the patient in one treatment, $5,000 for two treatments, $2,500 for three treatments and down to $306 at which time the doctor would begin to pay the patient for each treatment session after that until the patient is cured, up to the full $10,000. Can you imagine how that would change the practice of psychoanalysis? No more 10 and 20 year case reports!!

However the agreement system for psychiatry and psychoanalysis is set and I can't do much about it *but I don't have to participate in it*, do I? You may be in a job which produces money for you as a function of your ability to *not* get the job done in a quick miraculous manner. Have you ever wondered why people look forward to 5 PM when they can go home or Friday when they can take the weekend off? Why is it that people don't want to stay on their jobs and keep doing it? I'll tell you why: people know their integrity is out in their jobs, they know they are literally killing themselves by drawing a salary in a win/lose game and they can't wait until 5 PM, Friday, and age 65.

So, transformation in business requires the courage to stand up and say "I quit! Nevermore will I make money in this way! I'll starve first!" But, beyond that, it requires the willingness to look at it all fresh and create it all from no previous model, because the old models do not work, are not transforming. That is, no aliveness is created out of the old business models.

Fundamentally, a transformed business is a you *and* me business wherein I can win *only* if you win. Your success must be experienced by me as my success. Now, that sounds good, but you must take it a step further and design the business so that not only does one person *experience* other's success as his own, but further that one is actually rewarded with money for other's success. If I trained you to do a job and you went out and did it, it would be fair for me to receive income based on a portion of your income, wouldn't it? This concept is called Duplication. In Duplication one first gains a skill and puts it to work in business so that it provides a service and creates a profit. Then when you have mastered that skill, take other people under your wing, teach them the business and when they are competent, set them free to do that business and take a percentage of their profits for life as a reward for having made them successful.

Duplication is the essence of a transformed business. It is the purest form of a win/win relationship in business you can think of. However, what the Mind does with Duplication is plug it into the win/lose system. It just knows that if someone is winning, someone else is losing and immediately asks the question "Is it me?" Another barrier is that the Mind would rather die than make someone else successful. In truth this is the same barrier as the first one, with a disguise.

The way lack of integrity in a person making money in a win/lose system manifests itself is through invalidation.

Therefore, the Mind sees Duplication or Cooperative Partnership (another term for Duplication) as a potential con and tries to invalidate the person suggesting the Cooperative Partnership.

Nevertheless, Duplication or Cooperative Partnership, is the essence of transformation in business. This will become even clearer as you read the rest of this section. I know you want to go to sleep, I know this is confronting, but if you will persist in reading, and if you will put these principles into practice, they will work for you also.

Chapter Four
An Ideal Business

Do not settle for less than your ideals.

I do not have what I call a "settle for" outlook on life. I am just crazy enough to think that life could be any way I want it if I am willing to be responsible for making it that way. In business that translates into an ideal business. I have an ideal business which serves as a template for this entire discussion. I want to outline for you the characteristics of my ideal or transformed business so that you can begin to formulate what would be an ideal business for you and thus begin to design it for yourself. First you must eliminate any remnant of a settle for philosophy. Don't settle for less than your ideals.

The first thing I look for in a business is *freedom*. For me, that means not working for someone else, which translates into owning my own business. However, I want to be free and that means not only that I am not imprisoned by someone else's business schedule, it also means that I am not imprisoned by my own business schedule. Therefore, my ideal business has flexible hours so that I can work when I choose and not work when I choose. Just as I do not want to be someone's employee, neither do I want employees. Partners, yes, but employees, no. Most people do not have enough confidence in themselves to create this kind of business and few people have a sense of purpose strong enough to allow them to succeed at a business which is so flexible. So, most of us put ourselves in a harness so that we *know* we will have to work. The price is freedom, a price I am not willing to pay, nor am I willing to exact that price from another person.

The second thing I look for in an ideal business is *income*. I want the opportunity to make money and a lot of it. I want no ceiling on the amount of money I can make. If I decide to become a multi-millionaire, I don't want to be held back because I chose the wrong kind of business, a business that simply won't yield that kind of income without loss of my freedom. Now, many people have the notion that money is evil. Money is not evil, it is fairly neutral. Only a person can manifest evil. I see money as a tool for whatever your deepest desires happen to be. In addition to a lot of money, I look for cash payment at the time of service so that there are no accounts receivable. I don't want to owe or be owed to by anyone.

The third feature I look for in an ideal business is integration into the fabric of my life. I want to love the work I do so much that I am doing it all the time, even when I take my business partner out to dinner. (By the way, my business partner is my wife, Jean.) I want the Internal Revenue Service to recognize almost all my expenses as tax deductible. I can name you a lot of businesses in which you can make a lot of money—for the government, that is. I want to keep the money I earn and I want to keep it without stretching the truth to the I.R.S. That means that I must live my business and anything I live, I insist that I love also. I love tax deductions.

The fourth feature I look for is the ability to do the business out of my own home. I don't want to drive the freeways during rush hours. I choose to get up when I want to get up, come downstairs and be at work.

The fifth feature of my ideal business is having no territorial limitations. I want to be able to travel the world over and do my business and I want the opportunity to open up branches (duplicate) in any part of the world where free enterprise flourishes.

I want people to join me in cooperative partnership and I want anyone with talent and ambition to be able to do this without having to invest a large amount of money. I want to work with people and their futures, not their money. So, the sixth feature of an ideal business is that it requires no investment of money.

The seventh feature I look for in an ideal business is that it is part-time. I want freedom and that means an abundance of money *and* time. I want the time to enjoy the fruits of my work and I want the time to express those interests I have which don't necessarily manifest a lot of money.

The eighth feature I look for is a support system. No one begins life as a sharp business person. These things are learned, so I want a cooperative partnership with people who know business, preferably my business, better than I do who will teach me what I need to know at no charge and I want to be able to teach others in like manner.

The ninth feature, and one that I must have in any business in which I engage is absolute uncompromised integrity. I want to be able to close my eyes with all of my money on the table and know that it will remain there. I want to *never* hear a word from anyone about how he or she lost money in my business. That means two things: (1) no risks and (2) complete integrity.

The tenth and final feature I look for is a good product or service. I want to supply people with something that they need and supply it at a good price. I want to be able to offer them a 100% money back guarantee and be able to sleep soundly at night.

If all of these criteria are met, you can be certain that you are conducting a transformed and transforming business, one in which people have an enhanced sense of aliveness as a result of being your partner or as a result of being your customer.

So, to review these characteristics of an ideal or transformed business, they are: (1) Freedom
(2) Unlimited income
(3) Integration into one's life, thus tax advantages
(4) Home based
(5) No territorial limitations
(6) No financial investment required
(7) Part-time
(8) Support System
(9) Integrity
(10) Good product or service

Design a business that achieves these features and you will have a source of continuing transformation in your life and you will have a tool to transform the lives of others.

Chapter Five:
Networking

The most powerful way to make a difference,
and make income, in business, is networking.

I use the term "network" to describe a group of aligned people in communication with each other. It has long been apparent to me that who makes the difference in world affairs is the individual. The only thing that makes a difference in changing the ways things are is a transformed idea, and the individual is the only vessel in which a transformed idea can be carried. What I mean by a transformed idea is an idea whose time has come, that is it is more than simply a good idea, but it is an idea upon which people are aligned.

The suitable vehicle for communicating a transformed idea is a network. In a true network there is no center, that is no individual is more important than any other individual in the network. Each person has access to those other points or individuals in the network with whom he or she has taken the time to develop a relationship. The beauty of all this is that distance is no longer an issue. Modern telecommunications has made a world-wide network not only possible, but a reality. Any individual can join the transformation network and any individual can create as many points of direct contact within the network as she or he chooses.

A network can be visualized as a sphere with many millions of points on the surface. Each point represents an individual and each point has *potential* connection with all other points. Also, each point will have *actual* connection with as many other points as she or he has taken the time to develop. Do you know that studies have shown that between you and *any* other individual there are no more than five people? In other words, if you wanted to get a message to someone of importance on the other side of the planet, you know someone who knows someone who knows someone who knows someone who knows someone who knows that person. That's incredible isn't it?

This applies to transformation in business by virtue of the fact that your power in the business world can be incredibly enhanced by developing a network of aligned people. The requirements for a network in business are the following: (1) commonality of purpose, (2) duplication of your business, (3) commitment to the success of others, and (4) open lines of communication.

Let's take an example. Suppose you personally sponsored six people into your network for the purpose of setting them up in their own business, part of said business being for them to bring other people into the business. If your six sponsored six, each of whom sponsored six and those six sponsored six and let us say the average person in the network required two months to sponsor six, let us see the number of people in your network at the end of one year and at the end of two years. To do this we simply multiply 6x6x6x6x6x6 = 46,656. Now that is a lot of people, but at the end of two years the number of people in your network would be 2,176,762,336.

Only a couple of people in the history of the world have approached aligning that many people in anything. I don't want to say that it couldn't be done again and I will say that the game would have to be very interesting. The point here is not for you to go out and develop a network of 2 billion over the next two years, but to simply demonstrate the potential of networking. If you developed a high quality product and/or service and devised a marketing plan to reward people for the productivity of the network they developed, set up a workable communication system and kept your integrity intact, you would have a business with incredible potential.

The potential of networking is that it provides a vehicle which people can use to fulfill their dreams. There are many many people out there in society with a lot of talent who haven't been as successful as they could be simply because they haven't found the proper vehicle for success. Networking provides that vehicle.

Chapter Six:
Free Enterprise

True free enterprise is consistent with the nature of all humans.

Somewhere along the way in the last 200+ years we lost sight of our vision of what free enterprise could be here in America. There was a time when each person owned his or her own business or at least had a very open invitation to own such a business. Now, a small percentage of the population owns its own businesses. It is still possible to own your own business, however the social environment does not support the idea. Instead the social environment supports the idea of having a "good job" and working for someone else. To me there is no such thing as a "good job." That is like a "sweet rattlesnake."

People carry on about how poor people should want to work as if working for someone else should be this great joy in life. At the same time, the opportunity for a poor person to create his own business has been absent for so long that entire generations of people have come and gone and what it can mean to own one's own business has been forgotten.

Now, it is tempting to find a villain somewhere who is responsible for all this. The great department store founders, the magnates of the automobile industry, great oil tycoons, all the employers of the top corporations could be indicted. In a way all these are pyramid schemes with one person sitting on top of a rigid pyramid structure with the masses working in the middle of the pyramid in positions from which it is very difficult to move up. It is unlikely that anyone is going to start as a janitor for one of Detroit's giant automobile makers and end up as the president of that company. I am not saying it can't be done. I am saying that the environment does not support that happening, that is there is not a *free* enterprise system but rather a *slave* or pyramid enterprise system. People are not motivated because the incentive is not there *and* there is no experience of ownership of the corporation. If you work for a corporation for fifteen years, for example, you build tremendous value into that corporation and that value persists for many years. Suppose you decide to leave. How much of that value do you take with you? Suppose you are incapacitated and can't work anymore. How much of the value you built into the corporation do you take with you? None, that's how much.

As I say, it is tempting to find a villain in all of this, *and* there is none. Do not forget that ideas run the world and individuals do not. We swallowed whole a set of ideas which produced the kind of society we have now. I am not saying we don't have a great society. We, in fact, have the most magnificent system in the world. And there is plenty of room for improvement. The economic structures we have created are not yet in perfect alignment with human nature and therefore it is incumbent on us to continue to strive until *free* enterprise is achieved. True free enterprise is in alignment with human nature. At the base of every human heart there is a desire to contribute to others and given the right environment and the right incentives, *everyone* is motivated. Let me be clear, I mean *every one*, no exceptions.

Now that seems absurd because we have this great mass of people lying around collecting welfare don't we? Are they included? Yes they are. I am certain that every one of them has, at the base of his or her heart, the desire to contribute, to make a difference. But you see, for generations the opportunity has not been there, not the opportunity to make a *real* difference. Oh, the opportunity to be a slave has been there (that is to have a job), but the opportunity to make a real contribution has not been there. Therefore, we have an entire segment of our population that is so certain that the opportunity is not there, that if you present them with an opportunity, the opportunity will not be "seen." These people are simply brainwashed and we must not villify them. Our job is to continue to offer the opportunity, certain that eventually the opportunity will be seen.

What is this opportunity? As I see it, the opportunity is a system of free enterprise and to me this means applying the idea of networking into business. Networking bridges the motivation/opportunity gap and makes it possible for individuals to make a difference in other people's lives. And this is exactly what everyone wants at the base of his or her heart.

A free enterprise network affords unlimited opportunity—no ceiling—*and* to take the advantage of the opportunity, one must actually go out and do something, that is create a network. And it isn't necessarily easy, because the condition, the brainwash is still there; the negativity, the rejection, the invalidation. The way the perpetrations of "business as usual" over the past 200+ years manifest themselves now is by invalidation of anyone who would dare to suggest true free enterprise. If you suggest hope to a person in hopelessness, the first thing you get is rejection. He will think you are trying to con him, to use him. That is the way the Mind protects itself, by thinking those thoughts.

Nevertheless, if you are beginning to grasp what I am talking about here, regarding networking in business, you will soon come to realize that it will haunt you. You will realize that your integrity demands that you participate in and offer participation to others in a true free enterprise network, even if the invalidation is painful for you. Change rerquires people willing to put themselves out into battle.

You may not yet grasp what I am telling you here. If not, don't worry. Just continue to read and it will become clear to you.

Chapter Seven:
An Example

Free enterprise networking is already real and working in the world.

This plan involves sponsoring several people into the network, supplying them with products and helping them grow in their new business, that is providing service. In addition, each person in the network sells a small amount of products each month to retail customers who are not involved in the network directly. To make this clear, I will use a graphic diagram.

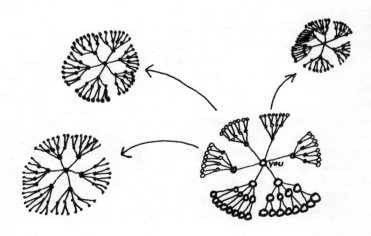

This is a Cooperative Partnership wherein each person owns his or her business and one's business includes all of one's "down line." In this diagram, you are represented by the center circle. You are brought into the business at the invitation of a sponsor, probably someone who knows you and trusts you. You in turn sponsor six people over the next two months and they sponsor four and each of those four sponsor two. Notice that this is a finite network, because when the network reaches a certain size and moves a certain volume of products, then the network breaks away from its sponsor. The person at the center of a network of this size is then known as a direct distributor and works directly with the manufacturer of the products and receives both his bonus check and his products from the manufacturer. Prior to becoming a direct distributor, one receives one's bonus and products directly from one's sponsor.

Income in a free enterpise network such as this one is determined by two things: (1) volume of products sold directly to the public and (2) service rendered to the other people in the network. The amount of service rendered to other people in the network is measured by the volume of products sold by the entire network. In a healthy business of this kind, the percentage of income made from retailing products to the public is very small, perhaps $2 out of each $100 earned. The other $98 comes from service rendered in building the business of the people "downline," that is distributors whom you have sponsored into the business and the generations below them.

The beauty of a business like this is that it is plastic. What I mean by that is that, like molten plastic, the size of the business conforms to the size of the person's thinking who is doing the business. Therefore, small thinkers have small businesses, medium-sized thinkers have medium-sized businesses, and big thinkers have big businesses. Therefore everyone is confronted with the size of their ability to think and another, invaluable element is introduced: personal growth. If you think you want a lot of success and you take on a business which can give it to you *and* you don't achieve a lot of success, you must confront those ways you are which keep you small. In practical terms, that means growth.

Needless to say, this kind of business has produced great wealth for many people. I am not going to give you exact figures because I don't want to blow your mind. The bonus system is structured so that tremendous income is developed as a result of "breaking direct distributors," that is helping the people you sponsor into the business to develop their own networks to the point that they "go direct" also. This is represented by the spin-off networks pictured in the diagram.

This kind of direct selling network free enterprise system is the cutting edge into the future of business. The advantages it has over the old department store concept is that most of the "middle men" are eliminated and people are given the opportunity to serve others directly. Whereas going to the store to buy a book gets you a book, buying a book from a friend who is a distributor gets a book plus the satisfaction of having supported your friend and his or her network of distributors. If you are the distributor you have performed a service for your customer, who is also your friend, and served the people in your network as well. You had a lot more fun selling that product than you would have had if you had stood in a store and waited for your friend to come and buy a book from you. You might have waited five years before that person came in and even then, so what? The profits would have gone to people you don't know in the management system of the store or, worse yet, stock holders who perform no service at all in the selling of the book.

I predict that by the end of the century stores will be all but obsolete. This change is part of the transformation of the world which is now in process. To me, this is an exciting age and it is a privilege for me to be able to participate in this transformation at the level of money flow (business).

If you want to see how this is applied to the book business, order *The Context Network, A Business of Your Own.*

Chapter Eight:
Heaven On Earth

Here on earth are all elements of heaven and those elements must be organized in your experience.

I am going to be audacious and tell you that life on earth can be heaven and first I want to know something from you. How do you *know* that you didn't live out a life on another planet, die and go to heaven and that *this is it?* In fact, you don't know that. If you will take that metaphor and *consider* it true, then you can create life on earth as heaven on earth. In fact, if you will think about it for a moment, there is nothing in a "heaven" which we don't already have right here in this life on earth. It is all available to you, you only need to take advantage of the opportunities in life. To the extent that you do not take the opportunities that come by, you live in hell—right here on earth.

Let me tell you what heaven is like. Heaven is having an entire planet on which to live. Heaven is having billions of companions in the game called life. Heaven is having challenges which stretch you out so that you can see how big you are. Heaven is being born and having a body to serve you and support you. Heaven is having people around you available to love you whenever you are ready to give up being right. Heaven is living in an age of transformation and having the opportunity to participate in that transformation. Heaven is having a condition of endarkenment in the world through which you can use your life to cut like a knife. Heaven is having people in the world whom you can admire and respect.

Heaven is having *nothing* given to you. Heaven is starting from the starting line in life and building your very own personality and your very own life out of the raw material of your own abilities. Heaven is being alive and having a dream.

I dream that my son will have all this to contend with, and more, as he grows into his full manhood. I have a dream that the world will have been better for him that I lived and grew into manhood and made the most of my life. I have a dream of freedom for everyone on the planet—freedom both within and without, both within the human soul and in the conditions in which we live out our lives. I have a dream that there will be a new economic order in the world and no longer will there be death from starvation. I have a dream that there will be a transformation at the level of relationships and that people will wake up in the morning and love each other, love their lovers, love their husbands, wives, children, neighbors, and especially love those people they don't know, not because of any reason, but just because that is the way life is. I have a dream that people will dare to step out of line, to be courageous, to make the contribution to life that each person deeply wants to make. I dream all these dreams and more, and much much more...I would literally lay down my life for these dreams *and* I would gladly keep my life and do whatever it takes to make these dreams into reality.

And I know that I am no different from you. I know you have dreams too. I know that you ache to make your contribution in life. I know that you want to give up the pettiness that keeps you stuck in the rut of life. I know that when it becomes real for you that you *can* make the contribution of which you always dreamed, you will step out of line, you will dare to appear foolish, you will operate in a space of no agreement, *you will confront and be responsible for the condition of the world.* And I know that you know that it starts with you, that once you know yourself and treat yourself out of your own magnificence you can begin to treat others in like manner.

And because you and I are thus related, I trust you, I admire you, I love you. I look forward to the future of our partnership together. And if this isn't heaven, there is no heaven.

Epilogue

Once again upon writing the last words to a volume, I am moved and inspired by the basic nature of human beings, inspired in truth by *you*, inspired by your vision for humanity, your courage, your dignity and your struggle with life. I know directly the difference you make, the gladness you have in being a human being and in being alive. And I know that you know that love *is*, that transformation *is*, and that you are both.

If you found value in reading this book, expand that value by sharing it with everyone you know.

Invitation

I invite you to correspond with me. You can reach me by writing in care of:

CONTEXT PUBLICATIONS
20 LOMITA AVENUE
SAN FRANCISCO, CALIFORNIA 94122
U.S.A.